Dawn or twilight?

Inter-Varsity Press

Dawn or twilight?
A study of contemporary
Roman Catholicism

H. M. Carson

Herbert Carson

© Inter-Varsity Press, Leicester, England

Universities and Colleges Christian Fellowship
38 De Montfort Street, Leicester LE1 7GP

First published under the title
Roman Catholicism today in 1964

Reprinted 1966, 1969
Revised edition 1976

ISBN 0 85110 389 8

Printed in Great Britain by
Hazell Watson & Viney Ltd, Aylesbury, Bucks

Acknowledgements

Scripture quotations, unless specified,
are taken from the Revised Standard
Version, Catholic Edition, published by
The Catholic Truth Society. For the
official teaching of the Church of Rome,
as contained in her documents, use has
been made of *The Teaching of the
Catholic Church* by H. Roos, S.J. and
Joseph Neuner, S.J., edited by Karl
Rahner, S.J. (The Mercier Press, 1966)
and *The Christian Faith* edited by J.
Neuner, S.J. and J. Dupuis, S.J. (The
Mercier Press, 1973).

Contents

	Introduction	9
1	The new Catholicism	15
2	Catholic Pentecostalism	29
3	By what authority?	39
4	The infallible guide	48
5	The appeal to Scripture	56
6	The evidence of tradition	65
7	The test of history	72
8	The sacraments	86
9	The priesthood	93
10	Transubstantiation	99
11	The mass	110
12	Ave Maria	120
13	Penance	136
14	Indulgences	146
15	Death and the hereafter	152
16	Can we be sure?	161
	Bibliography	170
	Glossary	172

Introduction

The commentator who wishes to give a fair assessment of modern Roman Catholicism will not find it an easy task. The present ferment within Rome, to which I shall turn in detail in a later chapter, makes it extraordinarily difficult to describe Roman Catholicism precisely. There was a time when definition was comparatively straightforward. There was a clearly defined body of doctrine interpreted by the teaching authority of the Church. The decrees of the Council of Trent and of the other major ecumenical councils, the statements of Roman canon law, the bulls and encyclicals of the Popes presented a solid body of teaching open to examination. Admittedly there were disagreements among Catholic writers but at the same time there was a broad general consensus. Indeed the proud boast of the Roman Catholic Church was that, in contrast with the fragmented condition of Protestantism, Rome could be counted on to present an unchanging front to the most searching scrutiny.

But today, as many Roman Catholics would be quick to admit, there are deep divisions within their Church. The conservatives and the liberals speak with very different voices. It is not simply that they have different emphases: on many fundamental issues they are diametrically opposed. Vatican II brought these divisions forcibly to the attention of the world at large. The blaze of publicity which lit up the debate on the floor of St Peter's showed how deep the divisions really were.

Those who try to keep abreast of Roman Catholic thinking are even more aware than is the casual observer of the depth and, at times, the bitterness of the conflict. I realize that some may feel that I am over-dramatizing the situation. For example, they may protest that debate within a Church is a sign of healthy growth, and even charge me with being rather churlish when I talk in terms of tensions and divisions! I can only plead in reply the tone of some of the disputants and the reaction of Pope Paul VI himself.

Pope Paul had to take over when Vatican II was in midstream. In the turbulent years which followed how often he spoke out against what he considered to be false trends and pronouncements. His famous *Credo* was clearly a counter-blast to what he believed was liberal deviation from Roman Catholic dogma. Preaching in St Peter's Square on 30 June 1968 he declared, 'We believe in the infallibility enjoyed by the successor of Peter, when he teaches *ex cathedra* as pastor and teacher of all the faithful. . . . We believe that Mary is the mother who remained ever a virgin, and that by reason of this singular election she was, in consideration of the merits of her Son . . . preserved from all stain of original sin and filled with the gift of grace more than all other creatures. . . . We believe that the mysterious presence of the Lord (in the Eucharist) is a true, real and substantial presence.' Admittedly he tried to steer a middle course, but it was obvious that, in his view, much of what was taught subsequent to Vatican II was subversive of Roman Catholic teaching.

Certainly a liberal like Hans Küng recognized this and he was not alone in his assessment. He quotes the French theologian Jean-Marie Paupert: 'The Pope has publicly and definitely put himself on the other side, the side of conserving superannuated structures. *Humanae Vitae* (*i.e.* the encyclical forbidding artificial means of contraception) is only one element in this decision, to which it is by no means difficult to add others: the papal encyclical on the celibacy of the priesthood (June 1967); the declaration on the body of St Peter (June 1968); the *Credo* of Paul VI (30 June 1968) and the massive attacks on the Dutch catechism. Though it distresses me deeply, I must declare my belief that, in view of the encyclical *Humanae Vitae*, we can regard it as certain that the door that was opened

10

for the first time by the Council has been shut again, even before the Church was able to tread the path to which it gave free access.'[1]

Another indication of the depth of the division is the tone of the debate. A book by an Australian Carmelite, Patrick J. Gearon, sums up the intense bitterness of many traditional Roman Catholics at what they feel has been a betrayal. He speaks of what he terms 'the liberal assault within the post-conciliar Church'. His estimate of the new theologians is bitingly clear: 'Efforts are being made today to replace the Church of St Augustine, St Thomas Aquinas and St Teresa of Avila with a new Church, the Church of Humanism and Evolution, the Church of "dialogue" with the world and the prince of this world, the Church of Teilhard de Chardin and Hans Küng. . . . Jesus had his Judas. Peter had his Simon Magus; Athanasius his Arius; Clement VII his Martin Luther and Paul VI has some Bishops in Holland.'[2] The publisher's blurb on Gearon's book cites an impressive list of papal commendations of his work, so presumably he represents quite a segment of traditional opinion.

Another conservative pin-points what is the real cause of divergence. G. H. Duggan dismisses Hans Küng's claim to be an authentic Catholic apologist. He writes, 'The root of his (*i.e.* Küng's) error is the principle – a principle that vitiates so much of his theology – that the theologian's starting point is Holy Scripture. This may be true of the Protestant theologian, it is not true of the Catholic who starts from tradition.'[3] I find this a particularly interesting comment as I encountered the same reaction in a televised discussion on Mary between a Belfast priest and myself. He charged me, precisely as Duggan charged Küng, with making an appeal to Scripture without taking into account, as of equal importance, tradition and the authority of the Church.

[1] H. Küng, *Infallible?* (Collins, 1971), p. 37.

[2] *The Wheat and the Cockle* (Britons Publishing Co., 1968), p. 75.

[3] G. H. Duggan, *Hans Küng and Reunion* (Mercier Press, 1964), p. 34.

All this makes for great difficulty for the commentator who tries to present a picture of contemporary Roman Catholicism and to give a fair critique. If he concentrates on traditional Catholicism he risks the indignant liberal reaction that he is a theological Rip Van Winkle who has been asleep for the last decade of tremendous change in Rome. If, on the other hand, he deals with the new Catholicism, he will run into trouble from the conservatives who will insist that the so-called progressives represent a deviation from the true faith of Rome and must not be quoted as official spokesmen.

One answer might be to write two books – one an examination of traditional Roman Catholicism and the other a critique of the new movement! But this is not really the answer. The line of demarcation does not run neatly through Rome, with conservatives on one side and liberals on the other. Some are liberal at one point and traditional at another. Take Schillebeeckx from the Netherlands, for example. He is in many ways among the liberal *avant-garde*. Yet his book on Mary is thoroughly traditional. There are always men who refuse to be labelled and whose ambiguous position defies classification. As a result a treatment of only one kind of Catholicism would simply ignore the fact that the frontier between liberal and conservative is at some points rather blurred.

What I propose to do, then, is to examine the dogmas of traditional Roman Catholicism. After all, these have not been repudiated and Vatican II still endorses the old doctrinal positions. At the same time I hope to take into account the new trends. But both aspects I want to bring to the final assessment of the Scriptures.

Let me add a word of reassurance. There will be no deliberate attempt to misrepresent Roman Catholic teaching, though in the present changing situation one group or another within Rome may feel that justice has not been done to its position. Then, too, I hope to avoid a mere attempt to score points. The issues are too serious for that trivial kind of treatment.

My aim rather is to view with sympathy the agonizing debates of many seminarians and priests and the bewilderment of many lay Roman Catholics; but to ally honesty and frankness with this sympathy. It is a false charity that ignores fundamental differences. Since it is the truth of God which is under discussion it would be a perversion of sympathy to fail to speak out openly for fear of causing offence. Graciousness does not necessarily mean compromise, nor does courtesy demand a guilty silence. Above all, my concern is that we might make the gospel of Christ the final touchstone. Ultimately it is neither my analysis and criticism nor the defence of the Roman Catholic apologist which counts, but the searching verdict of the Word of God.

1

The new Catholicism

The present troubles in Rome represent the second crisis of the century. The nineteenth century had seen the impact on the Protestant Churches of the higher critical approach to Scripture and of the resultant liberalism, with its implicit or explicit denial of many of the miraculous elements in the biblical revelation. With the dawn of the twentieth century the modernist movement emerged in Rome – in fact the term 'modernism' was in the first place applied to the liberal movement within Rome, and subsequently applied in Protestant circles.

The surge of modernism however was short-lived. Pius X did not face the widespread revolt which Paul VI was to face sixty years later. He was therefore able to act with firmness. Modernist teaching was condemned in 1907 in the encyclical *Pascendi Dominici Gregis*, and in 1910 the anti-modernist oath was imposed on the clergy. The movement was suppressed, though conservative Catholics would claim that it went underground only to reappear later as the new Catholicism. It is only fair to add that the present day progressives would deny this, though a consideration of the differences between the two might indicate that there is some weight in the accusation of the conservatives.

The reaction against modernism continued as late as the pontificate of Pius XII. In the encyclical *Humani Generis* issued in 1950 he maintained the authority of the Pope's teaching office. While admitting the difference between a papal utterance which claimed to be infallible and his general teaching authority, he insisted that when the Pope has declared himself on any issue the subject is no longer open to debate by the theologians. He

15

concluded, 'We are fully satisfied that the majority of Catholic teachers, employed in universities, or seminaries, or religious houses of study, are untouched by these errors; errors which have spread abroad, openly or in secret guise, as the result of an itch for modernity, or indiscreet zeal. But we know that up-to-date speculation of this kind may easily attract the unwary; better to deal promptly with the first symptoms than to seek remedies later on for a disease now firmly established.'[1]

It was Pope John who really opened the door to the progressives. He did this not only by convening the Second Vatican Council which provided them with a forum for expounding their views, but even more by his statement at the opening of the council: 'The substance of the ancient doctrine of the deposit of faith is one thing, and the way in which it is presented is another.'[2] In other words, the actual dogma is one thing and its expression is another. From the progressives' standpoint this was a welcome concession for, in Daniel O'Hanlon's words, 'he finally laid to rest the fear that had persisted among many Catholic theologians and churchmen since the modernist crisis at the beginning of the century. They had been afraid that if they tampered with traditional formulae the orthodoxy of their content would invariably be endangered.'[3]

Paul VI, John's successor, was to spend much of his energy trying to stem the consequences of this opening afforded to the progressives. He spoke out clearly in his encyclical on the eucharist, the *Mysterium Fidei*, issued during the course of Vatican II and after the progressives had chalked up victories in the debate on the liturgy and in the Constitution on the Sacred Liturgy, which was the first major document issued by the council. He expressed his anxiety about the spread of teaching which was minimising Roman Catholic dogma and reminded the faithful that the formulae of the Council of Trent,[4]

[1] Paragraph 40.

[2] W. M. Abbot & J. Gallagher (Eds), *The Documents of Vatican II* (Geoffrey Chapman, 1966), p. 715.

[3] *Concilium*, April 1966, p. 53.

[4] The Roman Catholic Council convened in the sixteenth century to counter the teaching of the Reformers.

16

'and others too which the Church employs in proposing dogmas of faith', are not subject to modification. He emphasized the position of the First Vatican Council that 'that meaning must always be retained which Holy Mother Church has once declared. There must never be any retreat from that meaning on the pretext and title of higher understanding.'[5]

It is against this background of conservative indignation and papal remonstrance that we must examine the general character of the new movement. We ask therefore – what are the aims of the progressives, what problems do they face and how do we assess them?

As far as their governing ideas are concerned we might sum them up under three headings – they aim to be biblical, ecumenical and loyal to Rome. These three aims inevitably lead to tensions and many would say that they are incompatible unless one or other is adjusted. The Protestant critic would claim that the progressives fail to be consistently biblical, while the conservative Roman Catholic would assert that they are not consistently Roman.

The strongly biblical emphasis is seen in their writings, where there is a constant appeal to Scripture. Hans Küng in his books makes Scripture his authority as he brings Rome under critical scrutiny. Even on a subject like that of Mariology a man like Schillebeeckx argues his case largely on Scriptural grounds.[6] There has been a marked resurgence in biblical studies among Roman Catholic theologians and at the popular level Bible reading is openly and strongly encouraged. There are, however, two areas where their biblical stress is open to question: first in the matter of the relationship of Scripture and tradition and secondly on the issue of the reliability and historicity of the Bible.

As far as the question of tradition is concerned the starting point for any Roman Catholic, conservative or progressive, must be the decree of the Council of Trent: 'The holy, ecumeni-

[5] Paragraphs 24 and 25.
[6] See E. Schillebeeckx, *Mary the Mother of the Redemption* (Sheed & Ward, 1972).

17

cal and general Council of Trent . . . receives and venerates with the same piety and reverence all the books of both Old and New Testaments – for God is the author of both – together with all traditions concerning faith and morals.' The First Vatican Council in 1870 followed closely the decrees of Trent and declared that the revelation of the gospel 'is contained in the written books and unwritten traditions which have come down to us'.

The progressives with their biblical emphasis have attempted to move away from this idea of two sources of revelation: Scripture and tradition. For them tradition is not to be viewed as a static body of teaching inherited from the past but rather as the living voice of the Church which in every age declares the inner meaning of Scripture. Thus they are attempting to give Scripture its position of supreme authority and at the same time to make room for the authoritative teaching office within the Church. But in so doing they have not really moved far from Trent, for a tradition which governs the sense of Scripture is really above Scripture in that it determines our understanding of the Word of God. They are indeed simply echoing the decree of Vatican I which was itself an explanation of the earlier decree of Trent: 'We, renewing the said decree, declare this to be its sense: that in matters of faith and morals, appertaining to the building up of Christian doctrine, that is to be held as the true sense of Holy Scripture which our Holy Mother Church has held and holds, to whom it belongs to judge of the true sense and interpretation of the Holy Scripture; and therefore that it is permitted to no one to interpret the Sacred Scripture contrary to this sense, nor, likewise, contrary to the unanimous consent of the Fathers.' [7]

The decrees of Vatican II did not make any real concession to the liberals on this matter but bound them to the demands of the Church's teaching authority, and emphasized as strongly as ever the important role of tradition. Here are some quotations from the Dogmatic Constitution on Divine Revelation:

[7] First Vatican Council, Third Session: Dogmatic Constitution on the Catholic Faith.

'Therefore both Scripture and Tradition should be accepted with equal sentiments of devotion and reverence.'[8] 'Sacred Tradition and Holy Scripture form a single sacred deposit of the Word of God entrusted to the Church.'[9] 'It is clear therefore that sacred Tradition, Holy Scripture and the Church's magisterium are by God's most wise decree so closely connected and associated together that one does not subsist without the other two, and that all of them, and each in its own manner, under the impulse of the one Spirit of God, contribute efficaciously to the salvation of the soul.'[1] The decree on the pastoral office of bishops takes a similar line, claiming that 'their teaching is based on sacred Scripture, Tradition, Liturgy and the Church's magisterium and life'.[2]

This whole approach fails to appreciate the New Testament emphasis on apostolic authority. The deliberate choice of Matthias and the sustained defence by Paul of his own apostolic position alike point to the centrality of this key theme of apostolicity. It was because of their unique position as eye witnesses of the resurrection – a qualification which clearly would not be possible in subsequent generations – that they were able to give the decisive, authentic and final testimony to Christ. In giving this testimony they were directed by the Spirit and they imparted a revelation which needed no tradition to supplement it. Hence the apostle John could write concerning the sufficiency of this apostolic selection of the essential truths of divine revelation: 'Now Jesus did many other signs in the presence of the disciples, which are not written in this book; but these are written that you may believe that Jesus is the Christ, the Son of God and that believing you may have life in his name.'

In a later chapter on the doctrine of the Church I hope to deal further with this issue of the relationship of the magisterium and the Bible. Here, however, it should be noted in passing that the qualifying of Scripture by tradition, and the subjection of Scripture to the teaching authority of the Church, make the present biblical revival rather sterile, because they fail

[8] II. 9.   [9] II. 10.   [1] II. 10.   [2] II. 14.

to admit that the biblical word is spoken to the Church and judges the Church. It must always be, for the Catholic, the word spoken in the Church, through the Church and interpreted by the Church. Rome's peril is then to have a Church which listens to herself and is without a master. She needs Luther's emphasis that 'the church is the daughter born of the Word, not the Word's mother'.

If, however, on the issue of tradition the progressives are bound by the successive decrees of the Councils, on the other matter – the infallibility of Scripture – they are increasingly influenced by the Protestant radicals. The traditional Roman Catholic attitude to Scripture has been to accept its unique inspiration and to attribute infallibility to the biblical writings. Thus Vatican I maintained that the Scriptures 'contain revelation with no admixture of error . . . having been written by the inspiration of the Holy Spirit, they have God for their author and have been delivered as such to the Church herself'. Leo XIII followed the same line when writing on biblical study: 'So far is it from being possible that any error should underlie the divine inspiration that such inspiration of itself not only excludes all error, but excludes and rejects it as necessarily as it is of necessity that God, the supreme truth, be the author of absolutely no error. This is the ancient and constant faith of the Church.'[3]

By 1920 Benedict XV had to return to the subject of the inerrancy of Scripture. He expressed his grief that among priests and theologians there were those who were rejecting either openly or secretly the traditional acceptance of the infallibility of Scripture. He insisted that it was not enough to say that 'Divine inspiration applies to every sentence, to every word even, of Holy Scripture,' if this were applied only to the religious content, for, he maintained firmly, 'It is wrong either to limit divine inspiration to certain parts of Holy Scripture or to admit that the sacred writer has erred.'

The attitude to Scripture condemned in 1920 has however

---

[3] Encyclical *Providentissimus Deus*.

become increasingly common. The destructively critical approach to the Bible which has characterized so many Protestant thinkers for a long time is now increasingly prevalent in Rome. Hans Küng, for example, speaks in many ways in a very biblical fashion and makes his constant appeal to Scripture. But he undermines this appeal by his acceptance of the approach of form criticism which leads to denials and rejection of parts of Scripture which he does not consider to be authentic. Thus he no longer makes his appeal to Matthew 16, the classic passage in the past for papal apologists; he rejects it. He does not believe that Jesus exercised the baptizing ministry recorded by John or that Jesus envisaged a missionary outreach. He does not believe that Paul and Barnabas ordained elders, in spite of what Acts says, because this would clash with his own theory that Paul's view of the Church was not institutional but charismatic, that is to say he was not concerned with an established order of elders and deacons but only with the exercise of the gifts of the Spirit.

Linked to this attitude to the Scriptures is their increasing agreement with the Protestant radicals who query the very possibility of making doctrinal statements which can in any objective sense be said to be 'true'. The thoroughgoing radical would insist that any doctrinal statement is simply an attempt to describe an experience, or possibly to recall the experience of the early Church. Indeed the New Testament is reduced to the level of a description of the early Church's experience of the reality of Christ. The virgin birth, the resurrection and the ascension are thus presented as 'myths' which must be stripped away if we are to understand the apostolic experience – which is the essential matter.

The historic Christian understanding of the Scriptures, and of those doctrinal statements expounding Bible truth, has been that these declare objective truths which are true in themselves whatever the verdict or response of the reader. The modern radical takes a different line. Truth, he asserts, cannot be presented in this static way. Truth is always a personal matter. It is always in relation to people. Thus to say 'God is good' is simply to say that God is good in my experience; God's goodness to me is a reality.

The fallacy in all this is that it begins at the wrong end. It starts with what man says about God rather than with what God says about Himself. If the New Testament is simply the religious self-expression of the early Church, then it is subject to the limitations inevitable for any finite mind trying to reflect on the infinite. But if, as Christians down the centuries have insisted, the Bible is primarily and essentially God's Word concerning Himself,[4] then it is not an imperfect attempt by men to express their experience of God, but God's infallible declaration which is objectively true.

This digression has been necessary to indicate the line along which many Roman Catholic thinkers are moving. Schillebeeckx, one of the leading Dutch progressives, comes very close to the radical position.[5] He claims that the doctrinal statement is true. But it is true only in so far as it is a signpost pointing along the road towards the greater truth about God. This truth however can only be experienced; it cannot be conceived or expressed in words.

This argument faces a dual reply. If the goal is lost in a fog, how can we be sure that the signpost points in the right direction? Then again there is the criticism mentioned earlier that he is starting from man's end. The Reformed contention is that biblical truth is not man's signpost but rather God's declaration made clear to man by the enlightenment of the Holy Spirit.

A further factor in the increasing approximation of radical Protestants and progressive Catholics is what we may call their 'incarnational theology' which is in fact rooted in a defective view of the atonement. Their thesis is that Christ by becoming man has sanctified the whole of life. As a consequence there is no basic distinction between sacred and secular, between Church and world. The fundamental New Testament contrast between darkness and light, error and truth, death and life is blurred if

[4] See Heb. 1:1; 2 Tim. 3:16; 2 Pet. 1:21.
[5] See Alting von Geusau, *Ecumenism and the Roman Catholic Church* (Sheed & Ward, 1966), p. 142 ff.

22

not extinguished. The Church becomes the sphere where men explicitly acknowledge the Christ whom others also implicitly acknowledge by showing kindness, unselfishness or concern for others, even though in fact they reject Him and declare themselves to be agnostics. 'It is possible,' says Kevin Mc-Namara, 'for the atheist in good faith to be numbered among those who love God and despise self.'[6]

Here is the old heresy of universalism so beloved of liberal theology. When Hans Küng writes: 'The resurrection of the crucified Christ which the Church believes and preaches is the proclamation of the resurrection of all men and of the renewing of the world,' he parts company with the solemn biblical message of judgment and the eternal separation of the impenitent from the presence of God.

Ecumenical Aims

We turn now to the ecumenical issue. Here we find the progressives very outward-looking and indeed it is in this realm that they have made such a marked impact on Roman Catholic thinking. We may query whether they are in a position to listen to other Christians in any realistic fashion in view of their commitment to the infallible teaching authority of Rome. But undoubtedly they seem to be honestly trying to discover what Protestants teach and indeed to learn from them. Thus Hans Küng wrote, 'Today we are interested in getting to know them because they too are Christians and Christian Churches and in a genuine and often better sense. And should we not be concerned with knowing our brethren?' And again, 'To get to know the others, then, means to learn from them, and as we learn from them we make ourselves better known to them.'[7]

This ecumenical stance however brings major problems in view of their other declared aim to be loyal to Rome. How, for example, do they accommodate the 'separated brethren' in view of the traditional contention, promulgated by Boniface VIII

[6] K. McNamara (Ed.), *Vatican II: The Constitution on the Church* (Geoffrey Chapman, 1968), p. 157.
[7] *Concilium*, IV. 2. p. 3.

in the papal bull of 1302, the *Unam Sanctam*, that 'outside the Church (*i.e.* of Rome) there is no salvation'. This, of course, is no new problem for it has often been debated in the past, but it is a particularly acute one for the progressives in view of their strongly held ecumenical interests.

An earlier answer to the problem was the plea of invincible ignorance. Protestants who were unable to grasp the claims of Rome would not be condemned, it was claimed, because of their ignorance. The assumption was that if only they could understand the papal claims they would accept them. This, however, ignored the fact that many instructed Protestants had studied the papal claims and understood them well, and it was for precisely this reason that they rejected them on biblical grounds.

Then came the idea that Protestants were in the soul of the Church but not in the body. But it did not require much acumen to see a flaw in this from the Roman Catholic point of view, for it made membership in the body optional. Yet it is membership in the body, which for Rome is to be equated with the Roman Catholic Church, that is fundamental.

A further suggestion is that the separated brother may have a desire for the Church even though he does not fully realize it. A similar contention is that the baptism of desire covers men who may not have submitted to Roman Catholic claims and may indeed never have been baptized. The fact that they have aspirations after goodness would for many modern theologians imply that they aspire after the benefits which baptism declares.

Hans Küng protests against this attempt to incorporate men against their will. He refuses to extend the idea of the Church to cover non-Christians, but then contradicts himself by extending the concept of Christian to embrace them. The net result is that he sees men being saved outside the Church of Rome and he is frank enough to assert that Vatican II finally abandoned the position of Boniface that outside Rome there is no salvation.

Mention of baptism brings us to the present line of argument in which the grounds for incorporating the 'separated brethren' are that they have been baptized. The theme 'brothers by baptism' is used enthusiastically both inside and outside Rome.

24

Indeed at this point we can see the impact of the progressives on the findings of Vatican II. The *Lumen Gentium*, the decree on the Church from Vatican II, sometimes known as *De Ecclesia*, recognized a close connection 'with those who are baptized and have the honour of the name of Christian, yet do not profess the faith in its entirety, or maintain union in fellowship under Peter's successor'.[8] The decree on ecumenism declared that: 'Baptism constitutes a sacramental bond of unity, linking all who have been reborn by means of it.' [9] *The Ecumenical Directory*, Part 1, gives detailed instructions to Roman Catholics on methods of furthering the cause of reunion at the grass-roots level of parish life. The basis of the approach is that baptism is 'the sacramental bond of unity, indeed the foundation of communion among all Christians'.[1] This enabled Henry St John to say at the Heythrop ecumenical conference in 1967 that non-Roman Catholics are within the Roman Church because 'they are sacramentally baptized even though, without realizing it, they live outside the visible structure and full organic communion of the one church'.[2] When baptism is interpreted in the very flexible way already noted, where 'baptism of desire' covers almost any conceivable response, we can see how widely the ecclesiastical net is being thrown. In fact this is simply another way of expressing the universalism we noted earlier, with its hope that all men will ultimately be saved.

In reply to all this it must be firmly stated that the sacraments have no meaning apart from the Word of God. Indeed divorced from the Word they become stumbling blocks. It is not enough to say that baptism unites, one must go further and ask the significance of baptism and its relation to the gospel of the grace of God. The apostle Peter reminds us (1 Pet. 3:21) that baptism saves 'not as a removal of dirt from the body but as an appeal to God for a clear conscience through the resurrection of Jesus Christ'. Simon in Samaria [3] had the ordinance of baptism, but because he was a hypocrite and had not truly repented he

---

[8] II. 15.   [9] III. 22.   [1] II. 11.
[2] B. Leeming, S.J. (Ed.), *Towards Christian Unity* (Geoffrey Chapman), p. 32.   [3] Acts 8:5 ff.

was rejected. The evidence that a man is truly born of God is not simply that he has been baptized, important though baptism clearly is, but that he exhibits in his life a pattern of obedience to the Word of God.

There is one further general point which should be mentioned in any consideration of the new Catholicism. It is one that has already been noted in passing, namely the clash between their biblical and ecumenical aims on the one hand, and their commitment to Roman Catholic dogma on the other. What makes this clash all the more severe is the claim by traditional Catholicism that dogma is unchangeable. Paul VI reminded the progressives when he issued the *Mysterium Fidei* that they must not imagine 'that although a doctrine has been defined once by the Church, it is open to any one to ignore it or to give it an interpretation that whittles away the natural meaning of the words or the accepted sense of the concepts'.[4]

The answer of the progressives to the charge that they are really the old modernists in a new guise is that unlike the modernists they are not aiming to modify the dogmas. The modernists tried to reduce dogma to the level of an attempt to describe a religious experience, so that while the experience is basically the same in each generation the mode of expressing it and the concepts used may vary considerably. The progressives claim, however, that they accept the dogmas. But they insist that because any formulation of doctrine is coloured by the historical situation in which it was made it is necessary to study it against the background of the period when it was produced in order to discover what in fact the Church aimed to teach.

With this approach even the Council of Trent yields new results. Thus Hans Küng will insist that the statements of Trent must be viewed in their context. The council had been convened in a time of crisis after Luther's revolt. It was not really representative, for the German bishops who might have understood Luther were not present. The controversial atmosphere meant that feelings ran high and any pronouncement was liable to

[4] Paragraph 10.

verge on over-statement. The result of all this is that for Küng, Luther and Trent were in much closer agreement than has been thought. Karl Barth rather acidly asked in reply, 'How must we explain the fact that this has, within and outside of Catholicism, remained hidden for so long?' Even more caustic was a fellow Roman Catholic who spoke scathingly of the Tübingen professor's Luther as a 'fairy tale from the Tübingen Woods'.[5]

We will be considering in further detail the progressives' attempt to deal with Catholic dogmatic teaching on the nature of the Church and on the claims of the papacy, but at this point it is important to note how fundamental this problem is for the new Catholicism. Indeed it is the issue which, if it is not resolved, must inevitably produce the dreaded schism. The conservatives dig in their heels and insist on the irreformable and unchangeable character of Roman Catholic dogma. They can appeal to the stand of Paul VI with his continuing insistence that dogma is not subject to modification: his sermon, *Credo of the People of God*, preached in St Peter's Square on 30 June 1968 was an unflinching affirmation of traditional Roman Catholic claims. On the other side the liberals are edging towards an even more radical attitude. Even Hans Küng, with all his attempts to be loyal, showed the direction in which the movement appears to be heading when he admitted that the Council of Trent was unbiblical in claiming scriptural warrant for the hierarchy. Here he went beyond his earlier line that Trent is essentially true in its teaching and suffers only from over-emphasis. This is an admission rather that it is not merely the emphasis which is unwise but the facts which are incorrect.[6] It came as no surprise when Küng went so far in his later books such as *Infallible?* or *Why Priests?* that Karl Rahner had to conclude that he no longer spoke as a Catholic but as a liberal Protestant.

Conservatives and progressives stand at the parting of the ways. Indeed some might say that some of them have already

[5] G. C. Duggan, *Hans Küng and Reunion* (Mercier Press, 1964), p. 13.
[6] See H. Küng, *The Church* (Burns & Oates, 1967), p. 418 ff.

parted company and while nominally still within the same ecclesiastical body are in fact following roads which are going in opposite directions. It is no wonder that very many Roman Catholic priests and laymen are confused and uncertain where to turn or whose voice to heed. It is the aim of the succeeding chapters of this book not simply to present a Protestant critique of Rome but to indicate a positive line where the gospel of the grace of God is the final arbiter.

2

Catholic Pentecostalism

In the autumn of 1966 and the spring of 1967 a new movement began to emerge which was to grow with incredible speed in the next few years. Before long it was numbering its adherents by the tens of thousands and was penetrating Roman Catholicism on a world-wide scale. It began among members of the faculty at Duquesne University, Pittsburgh in the USA. They had been deeply influenced by the account of a Pentecostal minister's outreach among the deprived youth of the New York ghettos, in his book *The Cross and the Switchblade*,[1] and although the movement was to differ at significant points from Protestant Pentecostalism, the very strong influence of the latter must not be minimized.

The movement spread first to other American Universities, to Notre Dame and Ann Arbor, before erupting as a widespread phenomenon in world Roman Catholicism. The main leaders in the early days were laymen, and nearly all of them were devout Roman Catholics before becoming involved in the new movement. In fact they saw the movement as heaven's answer to Pope John's prayer before Vatican II for a renewal of the wonders of Pentecost! It is not surprising, therefore, that they emphasize loyalty to Rome, and strongly deprecate any suggestion of secession. They see themselves as the agents of renewal in the Church rather than as the authors of schism. Indeed they would go further and claim that they are a unifying force, which can restore fellowship between the divided groups of modern Catholicism. There is a common experience which may unite both the theological left and right as well as the

[1] D. Wilkerson, *The Cross and the Switchblade* (Spire, 1964).

moderate middle-of-the-road theologians. It is not surprising therefore to find that they earned warm commendation from Pope Paul.

The firm commitment to Rome also explains their somewhat guarded attitude to Protestant Pentecostalism. While fully acknowledging their debt to the latter they are anxious to avoid some of what they judge to be its excessive emotionalism. Furthermore the biblical fundamentalism which has been the milieu of the Protestant Pentecostal is not acceptable to the Roman Catholic with his continuing view of the authority of the Church. So they distinguish between classical and neopentecostalism on the one side and the movement in Rome which they prefer to designate as the charismatic renewal.[2]

Before examining some of the distinctive characteristics of the movement it is necessary to digress in order to face the inevitable objection that any criticism of a claim to spiritual experience runs counter to Paul's warning, 'Do not quench the Spirit, do not despise prophesying' (1 Thes. 5:19–20). To this the immediate reply might well be that Paul does not stop at that point but adds a most important piece of exhortation: 'but test everything.' It is in the same vein that John urges us, 'Beloved do not believe every spirit, but test the spirits to see whether they are of God' (1 Jn. 4:1). It is no mark of submission to the Holy Spirit to accept any and every claim. We are called to exercise spiritual discernment.

There are plain reasons for the necessity of such discernment, for there are not only true experiences but spurious ones. A man may truly be moved by the Spirit of God, but he may also be deceived. Demonic activity is a factor which is taken seriously in the New Testament, more especially as Satan sometimes disguises himself as an angel of light (2 Cor. 11:14) and appears in such a plausible way that there is a possibility of his deceiving even the elect (Mt. 24:24; Mk. 13:22).

Apart from demonic activity there is also the potent factor of suggestion. We are not constituted as isolated individuals.

[2] T. Flynn, *The Charismatic Renewal and the Irish Experience* (Hodder & Stoughton, 1974), p. 28.

We belong together as human beings, as members of families, as members of other human groups, as members of the people of God. In these various shared relationships we are not only influenced by individuals, but also by the general patterns of community conduct, or by the prevailing climate of opinion. Often we conform to social habits or adopt a current attitude without realizing that we have not thought out the issue for ourselves. So, too, in the religious realm, it is possible to be so affected by others, or by a widespread movement, that we react in certain ways which we interpret as our new spiritual experience, but which may possibly be explained as the result of group suggestion.

There is a further important distinction which needs to be made in the area of specifically Christian experience. It is the distinction between the experience as such, and the explanation we give. Take for example the basic Christian experience of conversion. A man from a completely non-Christian background and with a minimum of knowledge of the gospel may come to a true saving experience of Christ. At the same time his explanation of what has happened to him may be very inadequate or even erroneous. As he grows in the knowledge of the Word of God, so he is able not only to appreciate his own experience more fully but also to explain it more correctly to others. We do not, however, leave him in error because he shows evidence of true conversion.

Now this distinction between experience and explanation continues to apply. Any experience is by its nature intensely personal and hidden. If it is an authentic work of the Holy Spirit, this will be evident in its out-working. So there will be the fruit of holiness in the life, there will be a concern for the glory of God, a deep love for Christ, a desire for fellowship with the people of God. It is with this in view that Jesus gives a practical test, 'You will know them by their fruits' (Mt. 7: 16, 20).

But a Christian who has met with God in a new way will not remain silent. He will want to share with others what has happened to him. He will want to explain his experience in such a way that they will see what he believes to be the truth which has

31

been a transforming word to him. But at this point the problem emerges not only for himself but for those to whom he speaks. If he himself has a faulty grasp of biblical truth, or if he is in serious doctrinal error, this will affect his explanatory statements. Instead of assessing his experience by the criterion of the Word of God he will tend to look at the Word through the eyes of his experience. Instead of being corrected by the Word he will tend to adjust the Word to fit his experience and the results will be serious.

As far as he himself is concerned he will be on the slippery slope of subjectivism on which the intensity of one's feelings rather than the landmarks of the Word of God is the standard. For others the outcome can be even more disastrous. If they have seen in him evidence of such a marked change that the new quality of his life commends his testimony, they will want to share his experience. If, however, they accept his explanation, which has now virtually become the new doctrine, they are accepting what is erroneous. The outcome is that they end in a cul-de-sac in which they either try to deceive themselves that they have had some deep experience, or else they react in disillusionment or even cynicism.

This rather lengthy digression has been necessary in order to guard against the contention that any criticism of a pattern of teaching, or perhaps even a rejection of such teaching, is of necessity a repudiation of a man's spiritual experience. I cannot read a man's soul. I cannot probe in such a way that I can tell whether or not he has met with God. The Holy Spirit's working in his soul is not open to my scrutiny. But the moment he opens his lips to explain, or when he puts pen to paper to expound his teaching, then I am not only entitled to test what he is saying, I am under solemn obligation to do so. Whether his experience is spurious or authentic will be evidenced to some degree in the quality of his life. But his doctrine is open to honest appraisal, and as always the standard of judgment is the Scriptures. The Bible is itself the product of the activity of the Holy Spirit. As the apostle Peter reminds us, 'Men moved by the Holy Spirit spoke from God' (2 Pet. 1:21). Surely, then, any claim to an

32

experience of the Holy Spirit must be open to an assessment by means of the Scriptures which the Spirit Himself has provided.

There are features of Catholic Pentecostalism which will elicit a warm response from any spiritually-minded Christian. The emphasis upon Bible study is one that can never be made too often. Then, too, the spontaneous praying marks a refreshing break with the rigidity of an unchanging liturgy. There is evidence too of a very warm fellowship, though it might be said in reply that any group which shares a common experience, particularly one which marks them out as quite distinctive, will also tend to be drawn close together. But even admitting this, one must still acknowledge that their love for each other does bear the stamp of New Testament Christianity. That I do not spend longer on these elements is not due to any desire to depreciate them. It is simply that in this area there is agreement and indeed ground for commendation. It is when there are serious differences that we must look more closely at the teaching being presented. As we shall be dealing in much greater detail with such matters as the sacraments and Mariology later in the book, we will simply touch on these issues in passing, in so far as they impinge on the Catholic Pentecostal position.

It is in the area of sacramental doctrine that we soon discover their commitment to traditional Roman Catholicism. Hence the Pentecostal doctrine of 'baptism in the Spirit' is linked with, and explained in terms of, the initiatory rite of Roman Catholic baptism. In the latter, grace, it is taught, is given *ex opere operato*, that is to say, by virtue of the performance of the sacrament. Thus an infant who obviously is incapable of conscious response, and who in Catholic teaching puts no barrier in the way of grace, has the stain of original sin removed and receives the gift of sanctifying grace. But this baptismal grace, it is claimed, is given in a hidden way, and in the baptism in the Spirit this hidden grace becomes explicit and open.

So on the one side there is the traditional view that the sacraments are the channels of grace by which Christ comes to men: 'in them, as it were, that humanity in which God is

33

perfectly manifested, is extended down the ages'.[3] Hence 'it is the same Christ in the sacrament as on the cross'.[4] The conclusion is drawn, 'If a sacrament is an act of God in Christ, a real act, then it does its work even if we feel nothing – provided we are not blocking it.'[5]

When this sacramental approach is applied to the pentecostal experience the argument is that the latter is simply a realization of what has already been received. 'In baptism . . . all grace in principle and "hiddenly" was given to us.'[6] The divine life was 'implanted in us at our baptism'[7] and so, 'baptism in the Holy Spirit . . . is precisely a prayer for the renewal and actualization of baptismal initiation'.[8]

At the first international Catholic Charismatic Leaders' Conference held in Rome in 1973 a draft statement of the theological basis of the movement was presented by Kilian McDonnell who had produced it at the suggestion of Cardinal Suenens. It was later formulated as a 'Statement of the theological basis of the Catholic Charismatic Renewal'. The claim is made quite emphatically that 'a theological-sacramental formulation . . . represents the most widely accepted view within the renewal'.[9] So Simon Tugwell's interpretation is not a personal deviation but is typical. This formulation is explained in a straightforward way. Referring to terms used in describing the baptism of the Spirit, such as 'renewal of the sacrament of initiation' or 'actualisation of gifts already received in potency', the explanation is given: 'These are all ways of saying that the power of the Holy Spirit given in Christian initiation, but hitherto unexperienced, becomes a matter of personal conscious experience.'

The sacramental interpretation is seen in the Catholic Pentecostal attitude to the sacrifice of the mass and the practice of

[3] Simon Tugwell, *Did You Receive the Spirit?* (Darton, Longman & Todd, 1972), p. 44.
[4] *Ibid.*, p. 42. [5] *Ibid.*, p. 45. [6] *Ibid.*, p. 59. [7] *Ibid.*, p. 63.
[8] K. & D. Ranaghan, *Catholic Pentecostals* (Paulist Press, 1969), p. 150.
[9] T. Flynn, *The Charismatic Renewal and the Irish Experience* (Hodder & Stoughton, 1974), p. 145.

the adoration of the reserved sacrament. In the early days of the movement in Ireland one of the leaders urged that a couple of the members should assist the work by spending an hour before the Blessed sacrament.[1] The conference of American bishops noted with favour that there was a growth of 'devotion to the real presence'.[2] In view of the claim that the strength of the movement is 'fidelity to the bishops and the Pope',[3] and in view of Paul VI's firm reassertion of transubstantiation it must be assumed that this dogma also is accepted – and, of course, it lies behind the practice of adoration of the reserved sacrament.

This sacramental view of the pentecostal experience is also seen in the explanation of speaking in tongues. Since the aim of the Roman Catholic should be the actual realization of the grace he claims to have received in his baptism, the exhortation is that we hand over 'one little bit of our body to God'.[4] The aim in view is expressed in terms consistent with the basic sacramental teaching: it is to allow 'the gradual permeation of more and more of our being by the divine life implanted in us in our baptism'.[5]

One can understand, therefore, the background of a typical testimony quoted by the Ranaghans:[6] 'I have found a new level of meaning in all the sacraments especially in confession and the eucharist.' Later we shall be putting forward a strong query from a biblical standpoint of the whole sacramental approach. Here it must suffice for the moment to notice how closely tied Catholic Pentecostalism is to traditional Roman Catholic doctrine. When we hear Simon Tugwell quoting approvingly Thomas Aquinas – to the effect that if there had been a consecrated host reserved at the time of Christ's death, we should have to say that he died also in the reserved host – it is abundantly clear that the background of his thinking is the dogma of transubstantiation and the sacrifice of the mass.[7]

[1] T. Flynn, *The Charismatic Renewal and the Irish Experience* (Hodder & Stoughton, 1974), pp. 7, 47.
[2] *Ibid.*, p. 128.   [3] *Ibid.*, p. 153.
[4] *Did You Receive the Spirit?*, p. 64.   [5] *Ibid.*, p. 63.
[6] *Op. cit.*, p. 70.   [7] See chapters 11 and 12.

Another issue which we will be discussing at much greater length in a later chapter is the place of Mary. Undoubtedly the cult of Mary occupies a very prominent position in Roman Catholic thinking, devotion and practice. It is equally clear that her role is still being firmly maintained within Catholic Pentecostalism. The Ranaghans quote testimonies to a deep devotion to Mary:[8] 'The Mother of God has become more special'; 'I have found a deep devotion to Mary'; 'I've taken up (the rosary) since baptism in the Spirit'. Perhaps the most remarkable of these testimonies is the description of a meeting in which someone spoke in a tongue. A Greek speaker who was present claimed that it was the Ave Maria in that language. As a result, the meeting took a strongly Marian direction. Not all were too happy about this, but, say the Ranaghans, 'we worry-warts were confounded and joyful to discover that the next day was one of the greatest feast days in the liturgical calendar. Our meeting the previous evening had not been a fearful diversion but an occasion. It had been a vigil, a preparation led by the Spirit for the feast that was to follow.' Now considering the fact that they acknowledge frankly that in the meeting 'the focus switched from Christ to Mary', it is hard to see how they can attribute this switch to the Holy Spirit, whose ministry it is to glorify Christ in such a way that He alone should have the pre-eminence (Jn. 15:26; 16:14; Col. 1:18).

It is not only in the area of testimony that one finds this devotion to the cult of Mary. Salvador Carrillo, one of the collaborators in the 'theological statement', expounds Mary's role on the day of Pentecost. The disciples he claims were 'presided over by the mother of Jesus to give life to the rising church'.[9] Just as she, by the power of the Spirit, conceived the body of the Saviour in her womb, so, it is claimed, she is part of the Spirit's action in giving birth to the Church. This is of course the dogmatic position of Vatican II, which declared her to be Mother of the Church.

A further dark shadow which hangs over Catholic Pente-

[8] *Catholic Pentecostals*, pp. 30, 68, 70, 178.
[9] *The Charismatic Renewal and the Irish Experience*, p. 171.

costal teaching is that of universalism – though, as we have seen in our study of the new Catholicism generally, it is by no means confined to the Pentecostals. However it is particularly significant in the latter case because of the steps in the argument which lead to the conclusion that all kinds of people may find themselves in the Christian's heaven without apparently having begun on the Christian way of faith in Christ.

Simon Tugwell frankly admits that he finds no theological basis for the doctrine of 'baptism in the Spirit'. But the reality of the pentecostal experience cannot be gainsaid. Instead of assessing the experience by scriptural tests, however, he reverses the procedure and makes experience the supreme criterion. So he comments, 'we read the Bible inevitably in the light of our experience'.[1] It is interesting that he sees the precedent for this in the traditional Roman Catholic attitude in which doctrine preceded exegesis. Hence he quotes Matthew 16:18, where the Roman Catholic view of the papacy determines the interpretation of the passage. A Protestant critic would reply that this is precisely his charge against Rome, that she so often subjects Scripture to dogma rather than bringing dogma to the judgment of the Word.

But Tugwell's elevation of experience as a criterion of truth leads him into even more serious error. He views the role of Roman Catholicism as being one of synthesis in which the various gleams of truth are brought together into focus. So he writes, 'All the fragments of our world are to be gathered into God's wholeness.' [2] But if experience is to be the standard, how are we to decide what is truth and what is error, what is to be embraced in the final synthesis and what is to be rejected? After all, others besides Christians have intensely real experiences. If experience is the final test then it is impossible to refuse any contribution if it is reinforced by a passionate testimony. Tugwell does not shirk the final conclusion, though it is one which parts company with the convictions of historic Christianity. He says quite frankly that in this quest for the final truth, 'Marxism, Zen, Transcendental Meditation, Pente-

[1] *Did You Receive the Spirit?*, p. 87. [2] *Ibid.*, p. 99.

costalism, all sorts of things, may help us on our way as we seek to enter into our inheritance of wholeness'.[3]

One is compelled to ask how this squares with the exclusive claims of Christ: 'I am the way, and the truth, and the life; no one comes to the Father, but by me' (Jn. 14:6)? How does it meet Peter's firm assertion: 'There is salvation in no one else, for there is no other name under heaven given among men by which we must be saved' (Acts 4:12)? Indeed one is entitled to ask further if the influence here is not so much biblical Christianity as the outlook of modern existentialism, where the intensity of the experience is the final criterion. The blind leap of faith which is rooted in irrationalism finds an interesting parallel in Tugwell's comment on speaking in tongues: 'It is a kind of prayer of the sub-conscious that we can quite deliberately use against our own recalcitrant minds and wills, thus defeating ourselves, in a way, for God.' [4]

Here is surely the approach of modern irrationalism rather than that of the Bible in which God calls men, 'Come now let us reason together.' In the New Testament faith is not a blind leap in the dark: 'Faith comes from what is heard, and what is heard comes by the preaching of Christ' (Rom. 10:17). In the miracle of the new birth the Holy Spirit renews the mind (Rom. 12:2; Eph. 4:23; 5:10). So we do not go blindly forward, assessing our progress by the intensity of our experiences. Rather, with an enlightened mind and in humble dependence on the guidance of the Spirit of truth, we aim to test all things, including our own experience, by the Spirit's own standard, the written Word.

[3] *Did You Receive the Spirit?*, p. 99.   [4] *Ibid.*, p. 71.

3

By what authority?

The basic issue in the debate between Rome and the Reformed Churches is the question of authority. For the Christian who is an heir of the Reformation principle, '*sola scriptura*' (Scripture alone), the final authority is clearly the written Word of God. But equally clearly this is not so for the Roman Catholic, not even for the progressive who accepts the decrees of Vatican II. What then is his authority?

It is here that many Protestants make the mistake of imagining that Rome simply adds tradition to Scripture to produce two sources of revelation. But this is only partially true, for at the apex of the pyramid above both Bible and tradition is the authority of the Church. It was the Church, says Rome, which gave us the Bible and it is her task to interpret the Scripture for us. It is likewise the church which pronounces which traditions are truly apostolic and how they should be understood. As Küng puts it, 'tradition gets the better of Scripture, and the teaching office in turn gets the better of tradition, because it decides what the tradition is and hence also what Scripture is'.[1]

But having said this, one must then ask what is meant by the term 'Church', and at once one is plunged into the current debate between liberals and conservatives. The traditional position may be summed up in the definition of Cardinal Bellarmine: 'The Church is a union of men who are united by the profession of the same Christian faith and by participation in the same sacraments under their lawful pastors, especially of

[1] *Infallible?*, p. 62.

39

the one representative of Christ on earth, the Pope of Rome.' Thus while Rome views the Church in its wider aspects as embracing those on earth, those in purgatory and those in heaven, she speaks in relation to the exercise of the authority of the Church in terms of the visible body on earth in communion with the Pope.

There has of course been development in the Roman Catholic view of the Church since Bellarmine wrote at the beginning of the seventeenth century. He was the heir of a tradition which stretched back into the Middle Ages. Then Roman Catholic thinking on the nature of the Church had developed in the context of life in the Empire; indeed it was often the clash between the claims of the Pope and the Emperors which sharpened the lines of dogmatic development. The Church in this situation came to be viewed as a spiritual empire with its graded organization of priestly officers (hence the term hierarchy) and with the Pope at the head as its absolute monarch. The stress was laid on structure and organization. The Church was an institution and within its organized life salvation was to be found. This was the idea which lay behind the *Unam Sanctam* of Boniface VIII. The Church of Rome was the means of salvation, the refuge for sinners, the ark of hope in the day of judgment.

Naturally the main attention of Roman Catholic theologians was given to the officers of the institution, and especially to the papacy for which increasingly sweeping claims were made. A comment by the French progressive Yves Congar is very apt. He complained that traditional Catholicism turned ecclesiology, the doctrine of the church, into hierarchology. It was in fact this emphasis on the institutional and organizational which led to the reaction of the nineteenth century.

Theologians like any other thinkers are influenced by the culture and the patterns of thought of their own generation. The nineteenth century was no exception. The rise of the Romantic movement influenced Catholic thinking on the nature of the Church. The Romantics were interested in the phenomenon of life in all its complexity, and so Roman Catholic

40

theologians began to look at the Church, not so much as a great institution, but as a body in which the divine life was the prominent fact. The Pauline metaphor of the Church as the body of Christ came to be the dominant idea in Roman Catholic reflection on the nature of the Church. But, as we shall see, the influence of traditional Roman Catholic thinking so modified Paul's teaching as to distort it disastrously. It is one thing to speak of the Church as the body of Christ; it is quite another so to stress the unity of the head and the body that the uniqueness of the head is lost, and the body acquires powers and qualities which belong only to the head. In other words Roman Catholic thinkers so pressed the idea of the unity of Christ and His Church, and so forgot the distinction between the two, that they ended by making the Church virtually another Christ.

The classic exponent of this position was Möhler, the German theologian. He wrote: 'Here is His Church, His institution in which He continues to live, in which the word uttered by Him continues to echo for ever. Thus the visible Church, seen from this point of view, is He who is continually seen among men in human form, who is ever renewing Himself, the Son of God who is being eternally rejuvenated, His permanent incarnation, the reason why believers are called in holy Scripture the body of Christ.' This leads him on to the conclusion, 'It is Christ who acts in the Church concealed under forms earthly and human. The Church has thus a divine and a human aspect. These two aspects exchange properties. The divine aspect, the living Christ and His Spirit, is the infallible element in the Church, the eternally sure: yet the human aspect is infallible and sure because the divine is not present for us apart from the human.' [2]

At the same time as Möhler was writing, the traditional emphasis on the hierarchy and especially on the papacy still continued, and found its embodiment in the decree of the first Vatican Council in 1870. The dogmatic constitution, *Pastor Aeternus*, declared 'that it is a dogma divinely revealed: that the Roman Pontiff, when he speaks *ex cathedra*, that is, when

[2] V. Subilia, *The Problem of Catholicism* (SCM, 1964), p. 28, footnote.

in discharge of the office of Pastor and Doctor of all Christians, by virtue of his supreme apostolic authority he defines a doctrine regarding faith or morals to be held by the Universal Church, by the divine assistance promised him in Blessed Peter, is possessed of that infallibility with which the Divine Redeemer willed that his Church should be endowed for defining doctrine regarding faith or morals: and that therefore such definitions of the Roman Pontiff are irreformable of themselves, and not from the consent of the Church'. For the benefit of those who are puzzled by the term 'irreformable' we might note Hans Küng's succinct explanation: 'It states quite unequivocally that no previous, contemporaneous or subsequent consent of the Church is necessary for an infallible definition by the Pope to be completely valid, and in particular that no consultation of, co-operation with or ratification by, the episcopate is necessary.'[3]

The two streams of thought flowed together in Pius XII's encyclical *Mystici Corporis*. Here is the same stress on the unity of head and members in the body, and here too is a firm insistence that the body of Christ is to be identified with the hierarchical Roman Catholic Church. He quoted Bellarmine who spoke of Christ sustaining and living in the Church in such a way 'that she may be said to be another Christ'.[4] Paul VI spoke in similar fashion in a speech at Vatican II when he declared the Church to be 'Christ's continuation and extension both earthly and heavenly' and maintained that 'Christ is our founder and head. He is invisible yet real. We receive everything from Him and constitute with Him the whole Christ.'[5] To quote a progressive, and incidentally to show that in this he is at one with the traditional Roman Catholic position: Yves Congar writes of the Church's being knit to Christ 'bodily and as by an extension of contact with His most holy body'.[6]

[3] *Infallible?*, p. 83.   [4] Paragraph 51.
[5] Y. Congar, H. Küng & D. O'Hanlon (Eds), *Council Speeches of Vatican II* (Sheed & Ward, 1964), p. 12.
[6] *Christ, our Lady and the Church* (Longman, 1957), p. 13 ff, 54 ff.

Pope John the convener of Vatican II was as emphatic as his predecessors on the uniqueness and supremacy of Rome. Reunion still meant a return by the separated brethren. The invitation was couched in gracious terms but it was still a call to return to what was claimed to be the one true fold. In his encyclical '*Ad Petri Cathedram*' summoning the council, he wrote, 'We cherish the hope of your return. . . . Observe, we beg of you, that when we lovingly invite you to the unity of the Church we are inviting you not to the home of a stranger, but to your own, your Father's house.'[7] He followed the same theme in his encyclical *Aeterna Dei Sapientia* in which he expressed the hope that the Vatican Council, then still in the future, might 'attract the gaze of the great majority of Christians of every denomination and induce them to gather around "the great Pastor of the sheep" who entrusted His flock to the unfailing guardianship of Peter and his successors'.[8] He was followed by Paul VI who declared, 'This Council, while calling and counting its own those sheep who belong to the fold of Christ in the fullest and truest sense, opens the door and calls out, too, in anxious expectation to the many sheep of Christ who are not at present within the unique fold.'[9]

In the decree on the Church promulgated by the Second Vatican Council there was a new emphasis on the Church as the people of God. This is indeed a biblical truth which is to be welcomed. But the truth was again obscured and indeed distorted by the continuance of the old stress which not only identified the body of Christ with the Church of Rome, but made that Church the channel of grace. The Church is still defined as 'a sacrament or instrumental sign of intimate union with God'.[1] It is 'the setting in which the communication of Christ's life to believers takes place; the sacraments are the means of their union, hidden yet real, with Christ in his suffering and in his glory'. Lest there should be any idea that Vatican II has departed from the traditional position it is firmly stated that 'this Church, founded and organized in this world as a society,

---

[7] III. 57, 58.   [8] III. 26.
[9] *Council Speeches of Vatican II*, p. 95.   [1] I. 1.

43

has its existence in the Catholic Church under the government of Peter's successor and the Bishops in communion with him'.[2]

Dutch Catholicism is famous – or for the conservatives, infamous – for its radicalism; but again we find the same exalted view of Rome as being in a unique sense the Church. Thus J. Hamer speaks of the Church as 'one vast source of grace' and adds, 'Where we find the totality of these particular sources of grace, there we find in all its wholeness the institution founded by the apostles, the Roman Catholic Church.'[3]

The idea of the Church as a continuation of the incarnation is still a dominant one. Vatican II contends that 'we must not think of the Church as two substances, but a single complex reality, the compound of a human and a divine element. By a significant analogy she is likened to the mystery of the Word incarnate: the nature taken by the divine Word serves as the living organ of salvation in a union with Him which is indissoluble.'[4] It is no wonder then that the decisive claim is made that the Church 'is incapable of being at fault in belief'.[5]

The basic position then is simply this: just as Jesus Christ in the days of His earthly ministry taught and acted and worked miracles through His physical body, so He continues to speak and act in and through His spiritual body, the Church. The analogy is pressed even further for just as we attribute infallibility to the teaching of Jesus of Nazareth, so Rome claims we must attribute the same to His body today. Hence to listen to Christ and to listen to the Church is one and the same.

With this view of the Church as the continuing incarnation of Christ the threefold office of the Messiah is expressed in the priestly and papal offices. Christ the Word of God still speaks, so it is claimed, in the teaching office of the Church, the magisterium. Christ the priest still offers the sacrifice in the person of the Roman Catholic priest who is presented as *alter Christus*, another Christ (see the encyclical of Pius XI *Ad Catholici*

[2] I. 7.
[3] Alting von Geusau (Ed.), *Ecumenism and the Roman Catholic Church* (Sheed & Ward, 1966), p. 116.
[4] Decree on the Church, I. 8.   [5] II. 12.

44

Sacerdotii), a position which is endorsed by the decree of Vatican II on the priestly life, where the priests are 'given the power of sacred order, to offer sacrifice, forgive sin, and in the name of Christ publicly to exercise the office of priesthood in the community of the faithful'.[6] Finally, it is claimed, Christ the king is present in the authority of the Church whether expressed by the role of the priest in the confessional or by the still existing claims of the Pope to sovereignty over the world.

The basic fallacy of this whole position has already been noted. The metaphor of the apostle Paul has been pressed to the point of serious distortion. It is true that Christ and His body, the Church, are one. There is a common life, for the Spirit of Christ abides in His Church. But at the same time there is a distinction. Christ remains the head. He is the Lord of His Church and it is utterly false to predicate of the body what belongs alone to the head. To claim infallibility for the teaching of Christ is simply to be scriptural, but to claim infallibility for His Church is to go far beyond the bounds of Scripture, and as will be shown subsequently, goes beyond the bounds of what has been seen in the actual, historical development of the Church.

There is also a curious inconsistency in what one can only call Rome's selectiveness in applying the analogy of the body. After all, we claim not only that Christ was without error, but also that He was always and unceasingly infallible and without sin. He was constantly infallible and consistently impeccable. How then can Rome claim infallibility for the Church without being committed to claiming a constant infallibility and also impeccability. If the Church is so united to Christ that she shares His infallibility, surely she shares it all the time and, in addition, the other point must be maintained that she shares also His freedom from sin. But not even the most ardent exponent of the infallibility of the Church would claim that there are no errors, no blemishes, no disfigurements, no sins in the Church. Certainly the apostle Paul did not consider the Church impeccable, for the vision of a Church without sin is reserved

[6] I. 2.

for the heavenly state. But the apostle Paul was not involved in any inconsistency, for he was not claiming infallibility for the Church either – this claim was one which developed centuries after the New Testament had declared the true nature of the Church.

The tragic consequence of this view of the Church is that Rome has left the Church without the divinely given check, namely the Scriptures. The Church herself becomes the standard of truth and there is no authority above or beyond to which she must submit and by which she must be judged. Yet when we turn to the Bible we find the people of God submitting to the prophetic and apostolic Word. The Word of Scripture does not emerge from the Church. It is not the word spoken in the Church and by the Church. The prophets stand over against the people of God and bring words of rebuke and chastening. The apostle Paul insists that his apostolic office is not derived from men but is from God (Gal. 1:1), and hence the apostolic testimony is a word declared to the Churches by which they come under the judgment of God. The Apostle John echoes the same emphasis with his refrain, 'he who has an ear, let him hear what the Spirit says to the churches' (Rev. 2:7, *etc.*).

Hans Küng has well criticized the whole conception of a 'permanent incarnation'. He writes 'Christ is the head and remains the head, which controls the body. The concept of head always carries overtones of the ruler. The body can only exist in total dependence on him. It is of vital importance for the Church that it allows Christ to be its head, otherwise it cannot be His body.'[7] He quite rightly sees that a Church which falsely identifies itself with the Holy Spirit 'turns itself into a revelation'.[8] This is certainly a far cry from Pius XII's *Mystici Corporis* and indeed from Paul VI's encyclical *Ecclesiam Suam* issued before the third session of the Council when he insisted, 'The reform cannot concern either the essential conception of the Church or its basic structure.'

A fair assessment of the present situation is that, in her essential message, Rome has not departed from her traditional

[7] *The Church*, p. 236.   [8] *Ibid.*, p. 175.

line that she is the one true Church, and that through her sacraments the grace of God flows to men. The decree on ecumenism may appear outward-looking with its friendly and welcoming approach to those outside Rome, but the old convictions are still as firmly maintained as ever. 'Our separated brethren do not have the benefit as individuals or in their communities and churches of the unity which Jesus Christ has wanted to bestow on all those to whom he has given re-birth into a single body. . . . Only through the Catholic Church of Christ, the universal aid to salvation, can the means of salvation be reached in all their fullness.' [9] Liberals may query the claims of Rome and especially of the papacy. They may turn to Scripture and find clear evidence to refute those claims. But constantly they are drawn by their committal to Rome back into the old dogmatic orbit.

The great need is for a radical departure on the part of Roman Catholic thinkers. Let a man make his present situation his starting point and his quest for truth will be stultified. Existing dogmatic pronouncements will so influence his mind that he will find it difficult to listen to the clear testimony of Scripture. Furthermore, as is evident with the new Catholicism, much of the energy which could so profitably be employed in searching the Scriptures will be dissipated in the unending attempt to reconcile an unchanging dogma with biblical counter-statement. The answer is a frank and honest return to the New Testament. Let the gospel in its simplicity be the starting-point. Let the apostolic testimony become the touchstone. Let the Churches come under the scrutiny of the Word of God. Let the whole structure of dogma and ecclesiastical office be submitted to the critical survey of Scripture. This is the approach which will lead men out of an ecclesiastical cul-de-sac and on to the King's highway.

[9] I. 3.

4

The infallible guide

To discuss the authority of the Church is to arrive inevitably at the issue which is the crux of the controversy, namely the claims of the papacy. In the past this was a controversy largely argued by Protestants on the one side and Roman Catholic apologists on the other. But that day has gone; not in the sense that a Protestant critique is no longer needed – it certainly is – but in the sense that Roman Catholics themselves are now embroiled in conflict over the papacy. Indeed one of the most biting attacks on papal claims in recent years has come from within Rome, for Hans Küng's *Infallible?* has all the vigour of the classical Protestant polemic. Whether his attack will continue from within Rome or whether, like others before him, he will be forced out, only time will tell. There is no question, however, that his examination of papal claims, emerging as it does as the climax of a whole series of volumes on the nature of the Church, is quite devastating.

The basic issue is this: how is the guidance of the Church given to the faithful? If the Church claims to be the final authority where do I hear her voice? The answer to that question has been formulated in many statements of canon law and in many papal encyclicals, but the most complete and detailed reply comes in the statements of the First Vatican Council supplemented by the celebrated decree of Vatican II on the constitution of the Church, the *Lumen Gentium.*

In Vatican I the emphasis had been firmly laid on the supreme authority of the Pope and on his infallibility in all matters of faith and morals. Vatican I, however, ended prematurely in 1870 when the troops of the victorious Italian nationalists occupied Rome. The sudden termination of the council furnished an argument for the claim that the decree was an open-ended one which needed supplementing by a further statement defining the role of the bishops and their relation to the papacy. This further statement came in Chapter III of the *Lumen Gentium*, but far from finalizing the issue it led to further controversy within Rome.

The decree claims for the bishops as a body what Vatican I had claimed for the Pope, namely the power to teach without error the doctrine of Christ. 'Individual Bishops do not enjoy the prerogative of infallibility. Nevertheless, when in the course of their authentic teaching on faith or morals, they agree on a single opinion to be held as definite, they are proclaiming infallibly the teaching of Christ.' [1] This means that when they act together, and in agreement with the Pope, and when they define a teaching on either faith or morals as obligatory for the faithful, they are teaching infallibly.

There is however a problem here even for a Catholic who is much more sympathetic to papal and episcopal claims than Küng is. Seamus Ryan presents it in his commentary on the decree: 'It is difficult to see how one can ever be quite sure that a particular teaching of the dispersed universal episcopate is infallible.' [2] For justification of his difficulty he points to the discussion on the subject of birth control. Judging by the tests of Vatican II the episcopal agreement for many years on this subject bears the clear stamp of infallibility. But the present debate indicates that very many would deny that this teaching is infallible. It is no wonder that his problem remains and he adds rather wryly, 'A dispersed episcopate which is infallible, but never quite knows when, is a puzzling paradox'.

One obvious way of avoiding this 'puzzling paradox' is to turn with an open Bible to a re-examination of the theory which underlies the claim to episcopal infallibility, namely the idea that bishops are in direct succession from the apostles. This

[1] III. 25.
[2] K. McNamara (Ed.), *Vatican II: The Constitution on the Church* (Geoffrey Chapman, 1948), pp. 208–9.

theory is maintained by the decree on the Church: 'The sacred Council teaches that it is by divine institution that Bishops have succeeded to the place of the apostles, as the pastors of the Church, whose hearers are listening to Christ, while he who rejects them, rejects Christ and Him that sent Christ.'[3] But surely the New Testament makes it plain that the apostles occupied a unique position. The qualification of an apostle was that he should be an eyewitness of the resurrection. This had to be fulfilled in the case of Matthias before his selection, and it was only the miraculous appearance of the risen Lord to Saul of Tarsus which qualified him to be numbered with the twelve. As the witnesses to the resurrection whose testimony was the foundation on which the Church was to be built, their role was one which by its very nature could not be repeated.

The theory of apostolic succession is a product of ecclesiastical wishful thinking, allied to a strange blindness to the tenuous historical evidence for any unbroken succession. But let Küng have the last word on this matter: 'We are nevertheless bound to point out that the attribution of infallibility to the college of bishops, based on the traditional unhistorical theory of the bishops' direct and exclusively apostolic succession, stands exegetically, historically and theologically, on feet of clay.'[4]

But the bishops have had to face a firm diminution of their claims from another quarter, namely from the Pope himself. Paul VI aimed to rule out any possible interpretation of the council decree which would accord them a status which might seem to compete with that of the papacy. Papal primacy and infallibility must be seen to be supreme!

Lest someone should imagine that in this Paul VI proved to be the reactionary in contrast with Pope John the progressive, it is good to recall that the latter took precisely the same line. He wrote very clearly in his *Aeterna Dei Sapientia*, 'All religious teachers – all bishops that is – must necessarily speak with one mind and one voice in communion with the Roman Pontiff'. This is because in his view: 'The focal centre of the

[3] III. 20.   [4] *Infallible?*, p. 70.

50

entire visible unity of the Catholic Church is the Bishop of Rome.'[5]

Paul VI did allow for the bishops' assistance but 'in ways determined or to be determined by the Pope'. In his explanatory note sent to the council on 16 November 1964, he reminded them that the college of bishops acts only with the consent of the head. Three days later they discovered how true this was when, in spite of a large majority in favour of voting on the issue of religious toleration, the Pope intervened and ordered a postponement. Events subsequent to the Council confirmed Pope Paul's insistence on his unique authority. In his 'Motu Proprio' issued on 17 June 1966, he proclaimed his rules of restrictions on the bishops' right to grant dispensations. He listed twenty areas which cover about 200 possible appeals for dispensation from Church law and declared that these appeals must be directed to the Vatican. One journalist writing in The Guardian aptly described this as measuring to the bishops 'in teaspoons some new privileges so that they may savour the collegiality for which they fought so hard during the four years of the ecumenical Council'. This decision came only six weeks after another significant one in which the Pope decided not to put five decrees into effect in June 1966 as originally scheduled. Once again the bishops must see where the final authority resides.

The decree on the Church was in any case quite emphatic. 'The college or body or bishops has no authority, if the meaning of the term excludes its connection with the Roman Pontiff, the successor of Peter, as its head, and unless the power of his primacy over all, pastors or faithful, be maintained in its entirety.'[6] 'In virtue of his office, the Roman Pontiff, head of the college of Bishops, enjoys this infallibility (i.e. willed by Christ) when he makes a definite pronouncement of doctrine on faith or morals, as the supreme pastor and teacher of all the faithful, who strengthens his brethren in faith. His definitions deserve in consequence to be called unalterable of themselves, and not by reason of the Church's agreement; for they are delivered with

[5] II. 18, 19.   [6] III. 22.

the Holy Spirit's assistance which was promised to him in the person of St Peter. Consequently they stand in no need of approval on the part of others, and they admit of no appeal to another court.' [7] The preliminary note of explanation appended to the decree makes it plain that no confusion must be tolerated between the office of the bishop and of the Pope, who is unique. 'There is not an equality between the head and the members but only a proportion between the two relationships: Peter – Apostles and Pope – Bishops.' The decree on the pastoral office of bishops continues in the same strain with a firm rejection of any minimizing approach to papal infallibility. Here is a typical quotation: 'In the Church of Christ, the Roman Pontiff as the successor of Peter, to whom Christ entrusted the feeding of his sheep and lambs, enjoys of divine institution supreme, full, immediate and universal authority in the care of souls . . . he holds the primacy of authority over all Churches.' So the decree continues its firm reminder that the authority of the bishops 'cannot be exercised except with the consent of the Roman Pontiff'.

It is this belief in papal infallibility which underlies the way in which Rome's claims are often presented to the potential convert. The priest may draw the contrast between the uncertainties of private judgment and the certainty of the infallible guide. In the past this argument could be presented with a greater degree of plausibility than is possible today. The fragmented condition of Protestantism and the seemingly unbroken unity of Rome were obvious to the most casual observer. The conclusion which Roman Catholic apologists drew from this contrast was that individual judgment leads one along a subjective path to an ultimate quagmire of competing opinions, whereas the infallible guide leads men to a common conviction as they share in the life of the one fold. This argument has boomeranged today as Rome is herself obviously divided. Possession of one who is claimed to be the infallible guide has not led to a condition in which unity in the faith is the hallmark, for the guide himself is assailed by dissentient voices who,

[7] II. 25.

while claiming to accept his guidance, insist on interpreting his statements even if he himself rejects their interpretation! The debate over the papal encyclical on birth control, the *Humanae Vitae*, is a recent illustration of this.

But this argument which would set the infallible authority of the Church against the uncertainty of private judgment requires an even more searching reply. We ask, therefore, how it is that a man comes to accept the infallibility of the Pope. Surely it is by an act of private judgment. Rome virtually admits this by her very approach. Here, for example, is the enquirer meeting the priest. The claims of Rome are presented, and the arguments are mustered. If he decides to accept these and submit, it is because he considers the arguments valid. But this is as much an act of private judgment as an attempt by a Protestant to come to a reasoned conclusion on any biblical issue. So we are really no further forward. The appeal to the infallibility of the Church does not deliver from the necessity of private judgment: rather, its very acceptance is derived from this same source.

Rome has, however, another rather popular approach. In the affairs of everyday life, it is pointed out, we consult the expert. We do not try to cure our illness ourselves: we go to the doctor. We do not settle our own legal problems: we employ a solicitor. Why, then, should we try to struggle with the complexities of doctrine and morals, when the expert is at hand? But if we think this through the analogy quickly breaks down. The doctor and the lawyer are experts because of their training and their knowledge. But when the Pope is set forward as the expert, it is because of his official position. This was clearly demonstrated at the First Vatican Council in 1870. One of the chief opponents to the dogma of papal infallibility, which was then defined, was von Döllinger, the eminent Roman Catholic historian. He was the acknowledged expert, while the Pope of the day was in no way outstanding for his learning. Hans Küng dismisses him as a reactionary 'without a trace of churchmanly or theological, critical self-reflection'.[8] But it was

[8] *Infallible?*, p. 75.

53

the Pope, not the professor from Munich, who won the day. And it still remains the case that it is the office of the Pope, as it is of the Roman Catholic bishop or priest, which confers authority, rather than specialized training or superior knowledge.

There is, however, a further argument in the Roman Catholic apologetic. It is maintained that it is inconceivable that God should have left His Church without a visible guide, and it is then pointed out that Rome alone claims to provide such an infallible leader in the person of the Pope. We might counter this by pointing out that to say a thing is inconceivable is simply to say that we cannot see how anyone could come to a conclusion other than ours. I may think it inconceivable that anyone could enjoy a holiday in the midst of the crowded deck-chairs of Blackpool. But that is because my tastes do not lie in that direction. So when a Roman Catholic says it is inconceivable that God should leave His Church without a visible head, we may reply that it is obviously inconceivable to him because he has come to this conclusion, but to multitudes of others it is quite conceivable.

We may then face another facet of the argument, as a further assertion is made that this conviction is not only a matter of personal opinion or taste, but a self-evident truth which emerges from the character of God. It is argued that, just as we would infer from the justice of God that deception by Him is inconceivable, so we may infer from God's love for His Church and His high purposes for it that it is likewise inconceivable that He should leave it to fall into error. A visible guide is thus seen as an inevitable consequence of the character and the purposes of God.

Turning however to the New Testament, we find that the two issues about which warnings are constantly given are false doctrine and evil living. Error in doctrine and sinfulness of life are to be avoided. Adherence to the apostolic gospel, and holiness of life, are to be our constant aim. Now, we ask, has God kept the Church free from sin? The answer clearly is 'No'. It is true that by the grace and power of the indwelling Spirit He

54

enables His people to resist the devil. But while we are in the world, perfection is as yet beyond our present attainments. Are we then to say that God sets greater store by orthodoxy than by holiness? Are we to say that God has not appointed an infallible means of avoiding sin, and yet has appointed an infallible means of avoiding error?

Surely the analogy holds good, for the one who is both true guide and sanctifier is not some man, but the Holy Spirit Himself. Just as our imperfect reliance upon His leading results in error, so our inadequate grasp of His mighty power results in sinful failure. Hence the call is to submit to His guidance and His control. As we do this, we advance in our knowledge and in holiness of life. Nevertheless, we must still admit that it is only in the final day of glorification that both knowledge and holiness will be made perfect. Only in heaven will both error and sin be completely banished. Meanwhile we press on, not in a hopeless quest, but in the sure confidence of the final outcome. And even now we have a foretaste, in the wisdom and the power of the Holy Spirit, which we already experience. But the quest for an infallible guide, like the quest for perfection in this life, is one which faces the emphatic 'No' of personal experience, of Christian history and, supremely, of Holy Scripture.

5

The appeal to Scripture

For the Protestant, 'What does the Scripture say?' is the ultimate question. For Rome, as we have seen, Scripture is only one authority, and not *the* authority. It stands alongside tradition, and together with tradition is subject to the interpretation of the Church. Yet it is none the less an authority to which Rome appeals, and we must therefore consider the main texts used to establish her position. These are Matthew 16:18, Luke 22:31 and John 21:16. Other Scriptures may indeed be used; but these are the basic ones.

Matthew 16:18
This is of course the key text *par excellence*: 'And I tell you, you are Peter, and on this rock I will build my church, and the powers of death shall not prevail against it.' Here, it is asserted, we have in our Lord's own words the commission given to Peter and to his successors, the Bishops of Rome. Here, it is claimed, Christ declares the apostle to be the rock upon which the Church is built. (There is a play on words in the Greek; 'You are Peter (*petros*); and on this rock (*petra*) I will build my church.')

Now before we examine the verse more closely, we must first of all insist that the Roman Catholic apologist establish from the text of Scripture all that he alleges to find there. Thus a leaflet for enquirers,[1] after asserting that the prerogatives of being supreme ruler and teacher of the whole Church were conferred on Peter, goes on to say, without attempting to prove

[1] E. R. Hull, S.J., *What the Catholic Church Is and What She Teaches* (Catholic Truth Society).

56

the contention, 'and they have been inherited by his successors in the bishopric of Rome'. In this, of course, we have simply an echo of the decrees of the first Vatican Council, which anathematized those who deny 'that in virtue of the decree of our Lord Jesus Christ Himself Blessed Peter has perpetual successors in his primacy'.

In view of the common tendency to glide all too quickly from one assertion to another without showing how the conclusions follow from the premises, it is important to insist that each element in the claims that are based on Matthew 16:18 should be clearly demonstrated. Thus to establish the full Roman Catholic position, four things must be proved: first, that Peter is himself personally the rock; second, that primacy equals infallibility (and this, we might claim, is a very doubtful equation); third, that Christ also conferred some privilege on the successors of Peter; and finally, that Peter was first Bishop of Rome. Even allowing for the fact that the fourth point would require an appeal to the remainder of the New Testament, it is undoubtedly true in the case of the second and third points that a great deal more would need to be drawn from Matthew 16:18 than is justified by the actual words. Whatever the text says about Peter, it says precisely nothing about any successors real or imagined.

But what does it say about Peter? Is Peter the rock on which the Church is built? In assessing the Roman Catholic interpretation of the verse it is good to recall an important Roman Catholic principle of interpretation. The second article of the Creed of Pope Pius IV deals thus with the interpretation of the Scriptures: 'Neither will I ever take and interpret them otherwise than according to the unanimous consent of the Fathers.' But judged by this criterion it is impossible to give any interpretation of the verse at all, for if there is one thing that is abundantly clear it is that the Fathers were far from unanimous in their understanding of this verse. Incidentally, if the Roman Catholic claim were really valid and this is the divinely-given charter of the Church which confers the primacy on Peter and the Bishops of Rome, it is an extraordinary situation that so

57

few of the Fathers, whose unanimous consent is so important, discovered the 'correct' interpretation.

What then did the Fathers decide about this verse? Launoy, a Roman Catholic scholar of the seventeenth century, compiled a list of the various interpretations in the early Church. Seventeen of the Fathers believed that the rock was Peter. Forty-four of them considered that the rock was Peter's faith, which had just found expression in his confession of Jesus as the Messiah, the Son of the living God. Sixteen of them said that the rock was Christ, and eight of them maintained the position that the rock referred to all the apostles. So much for the unanimous consent of the Fathers! If we are to accept the majority verdict then it is Peter's faith which is to be preferred, and certainly not Peter himself.

Of particular interest is the position of Augustine, the great theologian of North Africa. He changed his mind as far as the interpretation of the verse was concerned. In his earlier years he had claimed that the rock was Peter: but when he was an old man he moved somewhat. He admitted that he had also interpreted it as Peter's faith, and his final conclusion was that each one should decide which of these two interpretations was the more probable. But how devastating this really is. Here, we are told, is the key text, containing, as it does, the supremely important commission to Peter, a commission which is vital to the very life of the Church. Yet Augustine not only did not see the Roman interpretation as being the obvious one, but in fact was not apparently unduly worried about which view was taken, for in fact the main thrust of the verse does not hinge on this particular part of it.

The most that Rome can honestly claim for her interpretation of Matthew 16:18 is that it is a possible one. But at the same time it must be emphasized that, whether it is the correct view or not, it was a minority viewpoint in the early Church. But all this means that a very frail basis is established to sustain a tremendous superstructure – never a very secure method of building. But if it is very dubious to draw from the text a doctrine of Peter's personal primacy, what are we to say of

58

the exegesis which sees not only primacy but infallibility, and sees not only Peter but his successors? If all this can be elicited from Matthew 16:18 then Scripture can be made to mean anything.

Hans Küng has pointed out [2] that this supposedly key verse was nowhere seen to be such in the early centuries. It was not until the third century that Stephen II, whom Küng describes as 'an early example of Roman authoritarianism', applied it to prove the pre-eminence of Peter. It was only in the fourth century that it was being used by Roman bishops such as Damasus and Leo to undergird their claims for primacy. Nowhere in the East was it interpreted in terms of Roman primacy, and neither in the East nor in the West was there any mention of the claim to papal infallibility on the basis of either Matthew 16:18 or Luke 22:32.

But if the verse does not mean what Rome asserts, what *does* it mean? At first sight we may feel that we cannot move from the fog of uncertainty into the clear air of understanding. What, for example, are we to make of the suggested interpretations which the Fathers have bequeathed to us? Are we to give up in despair? In fact there is no need for this for if we look at these varied interpretations we will find that they are not so different after all. As we have seen there is a play on words in the verse. The name given by Jesus to Simon was in the Aramaic language, *cephas*, meaning 'a stone'. The Greek equivalent is *petros*, which is used here instead of his Jewish name Simon: 'You are Peter' (*petros*). 'On this rock' – the Greek word is the feminine word *petra*, hence we can see the play on the words – 'I will build my church.'

But the Peter to whom Jesus is speaking is the one who has just made his great confession that Jesus is the Christ, the Son of the living God. Thus whether we interpret the 'rock' as Peter witnessing, or as the witness Peter makes, or as the content of Peter's witness (*i.e.* that Jesus is the Christ), we are still reaching the same point. In fact the various interpretations converge

[2] *Infallible?*, p. 91.

on Paul's statement, 'No other foundation can any one lay than that which is laid, which is Jesus Christ' (1 Cor. 3:11).

What Jesus is saying is that the foundation of the Church is the apostolic testimony to Him as the Christ. That apostolic testimony, expressed here by Peter, has found its permanent form in the New Testament. In other words the foundation of the Church is the Lord Jesus Christ revealed to us in the testimony of the Scriptures.

Far from Rome's being on the right lines by according to Peter a special jurisdiction, she completely misinterprets the verse, which is asserting precisely the opposite, namely the Lord's own jurisdiction – 'I will build *my* church'. The Church is His, because in the eternal plan of God she has been given to Him (Jn. 17:2, 6, 9, *etc.*). The Church is His, because she is redeemed by His precious blood (Jn. 10:11; Acts 20:28; Eph. 5:25). Christ Himself is the sole head of the Church. Neither Pope nor prelate nor prince must be allowed to usurp His prerogatives. Indeed the elders must be careful lest they lord it over His heritage (1 Pet. 5:3), for the chief pastor is Christ Himself.

Here is a word also to encourage us in difficult days, 'I will build my church.' There is no doubt about the outcome of His work. 'All that the Father gives me will come to me,' (Jn. 6:37). The powers of hell may be thrown against the Church of the first-born, but victory for the people of God is sure, for the builder is the one who has already defeated Satan and will one day crush him forever beneath His feet: 'The gates of hades shall not prevail.' Like Peter we can say with thankfulness, with confidence, and in a spirit of adoring worship, 'You are the Christ the Son of the living God.'

Luke 22:31, 32

These verses read as follows: 'Simon, Simon, behold, Satan demanded to have you, that he might sift you like wheat, but I have prayed for you that your faith may not fail; and when you have turned again, strengthen your brethren.' But again the passage will hardly bear the weight which Rome rests upon it.

Is it really true that Christ singles out Peter, and speaks of praying for him in particular ('I have prayed for *thee*') because of Peter's special position as head of the Church? Surely, if context means anything, Peter is being singled out because of his impending failure. Thus in verse 34 the Lord speaks quite definitely of Peter's threefold denial. Furthermore it is important to note that this warning follows Peter's confident assertion in verse 33 that he is ready to die for Christ. This was an assertion which he made repeatedly, and which he must afterwards have recalled, in his hour of failure, with bitterness of soul.

But when a man is supremely self-confident, and then fails dismally, he is obviously liable to lose all confidence in himself. It is a short step from being self-assured to being utterly despondent and, indeed, despairing. How gracious, then, is the Lord who, as He speaks of Peter's failure, speaks also of His prayer for Peter, that his faith may not fail, and indeed that, through the humbling experience of denying the Lord, he may emerge to a new ministry of strengthening his brethren. His own failure, and the Lord's forgiveness, will give him a fresh word of hope for others who, like him, deny their Lord. It is something of an echo of David who in his hour of penitence looks forward to renewed fruitfulness, and a fruitfulness at that which springs from the very ground of his failure. 'Then I will teach transgressors thy ways, and sinners will return to thee.' [3] This ministry of the restored backslider would be Peter's in a special way.

It should be added that no special significance can be read into the commission 'strengthen your brethren', for this verb in the New Testament is not confined to Peter, as in the Roman Catholic interpretation. It is used of Paul's work [4] and, indeed, Paul uses it himself of his own ministry.[5] The strengthening of the brethren is not therefore the activity of one who has jurisdiction over them. It is rather the contribution of one who by grace has been raised from a sinful denial of his Lord, to a place of blessing.

[3] Ps. 51 (50):13. [4] Acts 14:22; 15:32; 41; 18:23.
[5] Rom. 1:11.

John 21:15–17

'When they had finished breakfast, Jesus said to Simon Peter, "Simon, son of John, do you love me more than these?" He said to him, "Yes, Lord; you know that I love you." He said to him, "Feed my lambs." A second time he said to him, "Simon, son of John, do you love me?" He said to him, "Yes, Lord; you know that I love you." He said to him, "Tend my sheep." He said to him the third time, "Simon, son of John, do you love me?" Peter was grieved because he said to him the third time, "Do you love me?" And he said to him, "Lord, you know everything; you know that I love you." Jesus said to him, "Feed my sheep." '

This passage, too, must be interpreted along similar lines. Certainly expositors in the early Church like Gregory Nazianzen or Cyril of Alexandria saw the threefold question as recalling the threefold denial. This seems to fit in with Peter's grief that the Lord should continue to ask. Yet he himself knows that his loud protestations in the past proved to be utterly hollow in the day of testing. Now as his profession is carefully sifted by the repeated query of the Saviour, Peter must have lived through the bitter experience of the night of his denial. But the threefold question humbles that it may exalt; it abases that it may encourage. The Lord still has a work for Peter to do (here surely is an echo of the prayer of Luke 22); for in his restored condition, with a new understanding, and above all a new humility begotten of his own failure, he is to 'feed the flock'.

To feed the flock is not however the special prerogative of Peter. Paul uses one of the two words employed here (*poimainein*) in his exhortation to the elders of Ephesus.[6] Indeed Peter uses the word himself,[7] and in so doing he does not designate the elders to whom he writes as under-shepherds. He, with them, is an 'elder',[8] and so he calls them to do what he has been commissioned to do, to feed the flock.

---

[6] Acts 20:28.   [7] 1 Pet. 5:1, 2.
[8] The Greek is *sumpresbuteres*, i.e. a 'co-elder'.

Elsewhere in the New Testament

A brief survey of the New Testament only confirms how unwarranted are the conclusions that have been drawn by Rome from the three passages which we have considered. Just as we have failed to find in them the primacy of Peter's jurisdiction, so we shall note the same pattern throughout the New Testament.

In the Gospels we find a persistent dispute among the Twelve as to who was the greatest. This surely was a completely irrelevant question if Christ had already settled the matter with a word which was so abundantly clear that none ought to have doubted Peter's position. But not only had the others failed to see it, but when our Lord rebukes them it is not because they are rebelling against Peter, but because the very question is such a worldly one.

The argument from silence is not a strong one if used alone; but in view of the strong supporting evidence, it is worthy of note that, while Mark and Luke record the incident of Peter's confession at Caesarea Philippi, they do not record Christ's words about the rock. Yet surely if this is the very foundation text of the Church we might expect them to include it.

In the Acts of the Apostles we find Peter being sent by the apostles to Samaria [9] in a way which would be inconceivable in the relationship of the body of Roman Catholic Cardinals to the Pope. But of even greater significance is the account of the Council of Jerusalem.[1] Peter takes part in the discussion, and has to explain his actions. But the chairmanship of the Council is in the hands of James, who also pronounces the findings. It would be easier here to demonstrate that James, rather than Peter, was head of the Church!

Paul's testimony is in the same direction. He sees Peter, not as the universal pastor of the whole Church, but as one whose commission was to the circumcision, just as Paul's was to the Gentiles.[2] So too Paul is quite prepared to stand up to Peter and rebuke him at Antioch.[3] It is because Peter was acting incon-

[9] Acts 8:14.   [1] Acts 15.   [2] Gal. 2:7, 8.
[3] Gal. 2:11.

sistently with his Jewish background that he rebukes him. He does not say to Peter 'if you, being the head of the Church', but 'if you, though a Jew'. When John wrote his first Epistle, the peril of false teaching was very real. Much of the Epistle is indeed a polemic. Here surely was the occasion to call Christians to submit to the infallible teacher, whose guidance would guard them against heresy. But John has clearly heard of only one teacher and that is the Spirit of God. There remains Peter himself. But how great a contrast there is between the tone of his Epistles and the tone of the average papal encyclical. The great swelling words of the latter with their claim to dominion over the souls of the faithful are simply not in Peter's letters.

One final brief word must suffice to deal with a subject which could sustain a prolonged debate, namely Peter's alleged bishopric in Rome. Paul writes to the Romans; but there is no greeting for Peter. Paul writes from Rome, but neither in the Epistles of his first imprisonment, nor in those written in Rome just before his death, is there any mention of Peter as bishop. Again we must admit that arguments from silence cannot be pressed too far. But there is justification for expecting some reference to his name or position if he were indeed the bishop of the Church in this city. Early tradition claims that he visited Rome and was martyred there. But a visit to a city does not make one a bishop there! Furthermore the tradition which links him with Rome, links him with Paul in the founding of the Church. Then again the list of bishops found in Hegesippus, Irenaeus and Eusebius gives, as first Bishop of Rome, not Peter but Linus. So we come back to where we began at Matthew 16:18. Just as we failed to find Peter's primacy there (or indeed elsewhere in the New Testament), so we have failed to find any prerogatives handed on to his 'successors'. In fact we would maintain that as an apostle, because of the uniqueness of the apostolic office, he could not, any more than Paul, have any successors.

6

The evidence of tradition

Having seen the failure to establish the primacy of Peter himself on the basis of Scripture, we turn to the position of those whom Rome claims to be the successors of Peter. Here, she teaches, the prerogatives granted to Peter are conferred upon his successors, the Bishops of Rome. We must ask, therefore, if the early Church recognized the Bishops of Rome as having jurisdiction over the whole Church as chief pastors of the flock of Christ. We shall find, however, that there is as little recognition among the Fathers of the jurisdiction of the Bishops of Rome, as there was of Peter himself among the New Testament writers.

It is significant that when Dr Ott is endeavouring to establish the primacy of the See of Rome, he has recourse to very weak evidence. Thus, while he claims that 'early on the Fathers expressed the thought that Peter lives on and works on in his successors',[1] the three witnesses he quotes belong to the fifth century, which is not quite 'early on'. Even more significant is the source of his witness. One is the papal legate at the Council of Ephesus; a second is a bishop of Ravenna in Italy; and the third is Pope Leo. But if we were to use parliamentary language and require these three to 'declare their interest', they would doubtless have difficulty in establishing their complete impartiality. We need, surely, to turn to witnesses who belong to an earlier period, and who are thus not likely to be so partial in their approach.

We begin in Rome itself with one of the earliest letters out-

[1] L. Ott, *Fundamentals of Catholic Dogma* (Mercier Press, 1962), p. 282.

side the New Testament, the letter of Clement, Bishop of Rome, to the Church at Corinth. There had been trouble at Corinth, and the elders had been deposed. The Church at Rome writes to remonstrate with the brethren at Corinth, and to call for peace. At first sight it might seem as if this is precisely the situation which the Roman apologist claims to be typical of the early days, with the Bishop of Rome aware of his divinely given rights and consciously exercising authority over other Churches. But a closer look will reveal significant factors which lead us to a completely different conclusion.

In the first place the letter is not sent by Clement personally, but by the Church in Rome. It is the authority of the Church, rather than the personal position of the bishop, which is the determining factor. Indeed Clement's name does not even appear in the letter; and the ascription of it to him is based on tradition. Lightfoot sums up the position. 'The later Roman theory supposes that the Church of Rome derives all its authority from the bishop of Rome, as the successor of St Peter. History inverts this relation and shows that, as a matter of fact, the power of the bishop of Rome was built upon the power of the Church of Rome. It was originally a primacy, not of the episcopate but of the Church.' [2]

It is also worth noting that the letter does not base its appeal upon some superior position enjoyed by the Church at Rome. It is rather a brotherly word from one Church to another, and the strong nature of its appeal is based, not on some claim to jurisdiction, but on the moral issue of Christian principle which is being violated. In view of the close links between Rome and Corinth, it was natural that such an appeal should be made. In view of the tone of the letter, it is no wonder that the appeal was heeded. But from this it is a most precarious inference that Corinth gave heed because they recognized in this epistle the voice of the Vicar of Christ on earth.

Turning to the second century, we meet the first of the many controversies which were to divide the eastern and western

[2] J. B. Lightfoot, *Apostolic Fathers*, I (Macmillan, 1890), p. 70.

Churches. The issue at stake was the date of the celebration of Easter. The eastern Churches celebrated it on the fourteenth of March whether or not this was a Sunday – hence the title given to the controversy, the Quarto-deciman. The Roman Church at an earlier stage had been prepared to tolerate the difference between eastern and western usage, but Pope Victor determined to take a stronger line and to demand that the quarto-decimans conform to the custom prevailing at Rome. Polycrates, Bishop of Ephesus, refused, and must therefore on the papal theory be accounted a contumacious rebel against the successor of Peter. What is far more likely is that he was simply a Christian leader who refused to be dragooned by one whom he recognized as no more than the head of a sister Church. Victor promptly threatened excommunication; and we seem to be in the realm of full papal claims to authority. But that Victor's assertion was by no means accepted is seen, not only in the firm and unyielding opposition of the Asiatic bishops, but also in the intervention of Irenaeus, Bishop of Lyons. Eusebius, the historian of the early Church, writes of these bishops: 'And their words are extant also, in which they censure Victor with unusual severity.' Of Irenaeus he has this to say, 'he nevertheless gives Victor much suitable counsel besides, not to cut off whole churches of God for observing an ancient custom handed down to them'.[3] Irenaeus in the controversy agreed with Victor's usage in the matter, but this makes all the more telling his rejection of Victor's act of excommunication which meant, in effect, his refusal of any alleged jurisdiction on the part of the Bishop of Rome.

When therefore we hear the often repeated quotation from Irenaeus, which exalts the position of the Church at Rome, we must interpret it in terms of his clearly defined position. Irenaeus, like many others, recognized the peculiar position occupied by the Church at Rome, as the Church of the chief city of the civilized world. He saw too the importance of the witness of that Church, for with the constant movement of

[3] H. J. Lawlor & J. E. L. Oulton (Eds), *Ecclesiastical History* (SPCK, 1927), XXIV. 10–11.

travellers to and from the imperial city, the Church there had a unique opportunity of keeping in touch with Christian life and thought throughout the Empire. Hence Rome, for him, is a stronghold of orthodoxy, because the constant flow of Christians from all the Churches brings a fresh and sustained witness from all quarters. Thus in Kidd's graphic phrase, the Church of Rome was 'Christendom in miniature',[4] or in Bishop Kerr's equally apt metaphor, it was 'a reservoir of orthodoxy'.[5] It was therefore the contribution of the Church at large, rather than any special prerogatives of the Bishop, which made the Church at Rome one to which Christians at large might appeal.

We will see in the next chapter the sturdy independence of the North African bishops in their resistance to Pope Zosimus, when the latter became the champion of heresy. But even before then, North Africa was notable for its resistance to Roman attempts at domination. The chief figure in this was Cyprian, Bishop of Carthage, who in his controversy with Stephen demonstrated his complete ignorance of any divinely conferred privileges held by the Pope. This rejection of papal claims is all the more striking in view of the fact that Cyprian is quite ready to accept Rome as the principal Church, much as Irenaeus had done. Indeed he is the first of the Fathers – he belongs to the third century – to accept the Pope as successor of Peter. Hence his firm refusal to accept directives from Rome is even more noteworthy. The very high position which he himself occupied in the estimation of the Church at large reinforces further our contention that the appeal to tradition in the third century is as fruitless for the papal apologist as is that to the tradition of the earlier centuries.

So we might go on, for the consistent testimony of the early Church points in the same direction, either ignorance of papal claims, or firm rejection. When we find the canons of the Council of Nicaea giving to Alexandria and Antioch a status analogous to that of Rome, we find a summary of this attitude.

[4] B. J. Kidd, *The Roman Primacy* (SPCK, 1936), p. 15.
[5] W. S. Kerr, *A Handbook on the Papacy* (Marshall, Morgan & Scott, 1962), p. 92.

Each of these centres occupied a prominent position and to each of them, therefore, is accorded a respect due to their pre-eminence in their own area. But it is important to note that the basis of their primacy is the same. If, then, Rome achieved a greater eminence it was simply the fact that the city was itself pre-eminent. This is seen further in the rise of Constantinople. When this city became the imperial capital, a second Rome, the Church there acquired a correspondingly important position. In other words Rome, and to a lesser degree Constantinople, basked in the reflected glory of their imperial surroundings. But this is hardly the same thing as a reflection of a commission from the King of kings.

There were of course other factors which led to Rome's authority increasing, one of which was a very worthy reason and the other one wholly unworthy. The element which contributed to Rome's greatness, for which Christians in Rome might well give thanks to God, was the stand of many of their leaders for orthodoxy. The most notable example of this was Leo, whose letter to the patriarch of Constantinople in AD 449 [6] was the basis of the orthodox formulation of the doctrine of the Person of Christ at the Council of Chalcedon. This did not mean that the early Church was thus prepared to accept every edict of the Pope. When a Liberius or a Honorius went into heresy they were rejected. But on the credit side, when in testing days men of the stature of Leo stood firm, the stock of the Church in Rome was correspondingly high.

But if the imperial status of Rome, and the greatness of some of the bishops, are grounds which we can easily acknowledge in trying to assess the rise to importance of that Church, the other major factor in establishing, not simply a position of importance, but one of pre-eminence, is one of which any Church might deservedly feel thoroughly ashamed. Forgeries at any time are despicable expedients, but when they are used by a Church to bolster up a position, then they are not only despicable but terribly culpable.

The two main forgeries used to buttress the papal claims are

[6] Generally known as the *Tome* of Leo.

the so-called Clementine literature and the false Decretals –
the title given to official letters from the Bishops of Rome. The
former group of writings probably attained acceptance because
they bore the name of one who was highly esteemed in the early
Church. But few, if any, scholars would load Clement with the
responsibility for a production in which legend and fantastic
miracle oust any pretension to historical worth. Their excessive
claims for the apostle Peter, and so for the city over which, in
defiance of the lists of Irenaeus and Eusebius, they make him
first bishop, are hardly likely to establish those claims with
anyone except the most gullible.

A more blatant example of forgery, and one that became the
prime factor in the extravagant claims of Rome, was the forged
Decretals. The collection was supposed to have been made in
the seventh century by Isidore of Seville. In actual fact they
were probably produced in France in the ninth century. Once
again there was a body of writing bearing an august name; and
once again it won acceptance. Apart from a collection of canons
of Councils, it consists of letters from Popes of the period
before the Council of Nicaea and also a collection of letters
from the time of Pope Silvester to that of Gregory II, that is
from the fourth to the eighth century. Right through the
Middle Ages, until the time of the Renaissance, these letters
were accepted as genuine. On them was grounded the papal
claim to sovereignty over the Church, and temporal authority
in the West, the latter based on the so-called Donation of Con-
stantine. The Renaissance scholars, however, showed up many
of these letters as forgeries, the ones alleged to be from the
ante-Nicene Popes being completely rejected. But here comes
the incredible position. While Roman Catholic scholars would
today accept the verdict which accounts the Decretals to be
clumsy forgeries, they still maintain the claims of the Pope
which were based on them. The foundation is gone but the
superstructure remains. Now whatever we may think of the
medieval Popes who with complete credulity accepted the letters
as genuine and made tremendous claims as a consequence, what
are we to say about those who today acknowledge the falsity of

the Decretals, but still endorse the claim? 'Well,' says Salmon, 'if a man presents a forged cheque, and gets money for it, it is something to say in his defence that he did not forge it himself; but if he were an honest man, as soon as he discovered the forgery he would give back what he had wrongfully acquired.'[7] But this is what the Popes of Rome have refused to do.

One final word may be added. The false Decretals confirm in an indirect manner the conclusion reached by the appeal to the Fathers of the early Church. It was a quite obvious fact that, because no genuine letters from the early Bishops of Rome nor canons of the early Councils could be found to establish the papal claims, recourse was had to forgery. When a man is driven to the desperate expedient of passing a forged cheque, it is an indication of the state of his own bank account! The false Decretals are thus an eloquent commentary on the utter bankruptcy of the claims of the Roman Catholic Church on behalf of the papacy.

[7] G. Salmon, *The Infallibility of the Church* (John Murray, 1914; abridged edn: 1953), p. 454.

7

The test of history

The facts of history are reliable friends of the truth, but they are equally relentless foes of error. So we turn to facts, as we continue our consideration of the basic Roman Catholic assertion that it is inconceivable that God would have left His Church without a visible head. To do this we need to ask if the Roman Catholic position, which we have queried in its basic assumptions, can be substantiated by history. The conclusion to which we are driven is that it cannot. If the guidance of the infallible guide is of such an essential character that it is impossible to think of the Church apart from it, then clearly the history of the Church must demonstrate the truth of the infallibility of the Pope working out in experience, or else it will show that the quest for an infallible guide is a chase after an ecclesiastical will o' the wisp.

In setting the Roman claims over against the facts of history, we shall propose three tests which the claims should satisfy, tests which no reasonable Roman Catholic can say are unfair. In the first place we have a right to expect that the infallible guide will be clearly recognizable, for to speak of a visible guide whose credentials are not completely sure is a contradiction in terms. Secondly, it is fair to presume that the infallible guide will act with reasonable promptitude when the faithful have reached an end of their own resources and are in danger of serious error. Thirdly, it goes without saying that the infallible guide will not himself be responsible for leading his people into error. These, then, are the tests which we shall consider.

a. The Credentials of the Infallible Guide

The Roman reply to this query seems at first to be quite simple and obvious. The Pope alone lays claim to the position of being the Vicar of Christ on earth. Furthermore, there is no difficulty in deciding where the guide is to be found, for he is the presiding Bishop of Rome, recognized and acknowledged by millions of Roman Catholics all over the world. To ask who is the visible head of the Church would seem to the average Roman Catholic utterly fatuous.

But while it is true today that the Pope is easily identified, both by his own adherents and even by those who reject his claims, yet it has not always been so. The history of the papacy is strewn with a line of anti-popes who have laid claim to the See of Rome, and so to the allegiance of the faithful. The Roman Catholic may well reply that the presence of a rebel, or even a usurper, in no way invalidates the claims of the rightful sovereign, and the fact that there have been ecclesiastical rebels does not in any way compel acceptance of their claims. Indeed, says the Roman Catholic, the true occupant of the papal throne is recognizable in contrast with the false claimant.

We are dealing now with facts; and so we must examine the most famous of these periods when there were two claimants to the papacy, *viz.* the Great Schism of the late fourteenth and early fifteenth centuries. In the year 1377, there ended what had become known as the Babylonish Captivity of the Church. For sixty-eight years the Popes had resided at Avignon in France where, naturally, they tended to be dominated by the French crown. Thus when Gregory XI returned to Rome it seemed to promise a new day.

But Gregory's death led to trouble. The cardinals elected an Italian, Urban VI. He however did not prove amenable to their ideas and, claiming that they had acted under duress (it was not the first time that the mob in Rome was a factor in papal elections), they withdrew and elected a Frenchman, Clement VII, who returned to Avignon. The schism continued with their successors until in 1409 the Council of Pisa, in an attempt to heal the breach, deposed both Popes and elected Alexander

V. The two who were deposed refused to go, leaving the farcical situation of three Popes. Pope number three had as his successor John XXIII (the same number as the Pope John who died in 1963).

Now while the two Popes reigned, one at Rome and the other at Avignon, Roman Catholic Europe was divided in its allegiance. Scotland, Naples, France and Spain supported Clement VII, while England, Poland, Bohemia, Hungary, Portugal and most of Italy endorsed Urban VI. Theologians and 'saints' were ranged in opposite camps. The Popes themselves were aware of the issues at stake and flung the most terrifying anathemas at each other. Who was the true guide then? Whatever verdict Roman Catholic scholars may pass today, it is an unassailable fact that at the time there was no certainty, for the Church was split asunder on the question.

Let us recall our reason for discussing this issue. The Roman Catholic apologist claims that it is inconceivable that God should have left His Church without a visible head. He claims further that it is a matter fraught with eternal consequences; for submission to the true guide is bound up with a man's eternal salvation. Now this schism lasted over fifty years until 1429. Considering the expectation of life in the fifteenth century, there must have been many who lived their whole lives during this period of uncertainty in the Church. They would naturally follow their priests' and bishops' advice. But inevitably many were wrong, for they were following the wrong guide; and they were wrong on a matter which concerned their eternal salvation. To say that, as long as they sincerely believed in the existence of the true, visible head, they could be excused their mistake is simply to say that the claims of Rome are an optional extra. Certainly the failure by a large section of Christians, not all of them either knaves or fools, to identify the visible head undermines the basic assumption that Christ could not conceivably have left His Church without a visible head. The answer of the period of the Great Schism simply is – He did!

b. Reasonable and Unreasonable Delays

The second request that we make, if Rome is to substantiate her claim, is that the infallible guide should act reasonably promptly. Of course it is quite obvious that no guide in any field of learning will give answers which the student can find out for himself. Instruction in any subject is not intended to be a substitute for hard work on the student's part. So we can easily concede the point that the Pope is quite entitled to stand back and let the theologians give their minds to the problems. Spoon-feeding in theology is no more appropriate than in any other branch of learning. At the same time it is equally true that a good tutor will not stand back and watch his student cling to a wrong position which affects all his subsequent thinking. Nor, when he finds his student floundering in a morass from which he seems incapable of extricating himself, will he withhold his assistance. It is at these points, when the student is either unable to make any headway or is going in the wrong direction, that we expect the tutor to intervene. Now when a similar situation arises in the Church, where there is a doctrinal impasse, or where false teaching or dangerously inadequate teaching is being embraced, are we not justified in saying that the infallible guide, if such there be, has a clear moral obligation to speak?

But has the infallible guide thus spoken out clearly when the situation obviously required an answer? The facts of history speak for themselves. They reveal his extreme reluctance to commit himself; they suggest that considerations of expediency rather than a conviction of his own infallibility were the dominant factors. From the possible illustrations of this hesitant attitude we select three – the controversy over the immaculate conception of the Virgin Mary; the acceptance of modern revelations; and the final promulgation of the dogma of papal infallibility itself.

In dealing with the dogma of the immaculate conception we are not considering at this stage the arguments for or against it.[1] We are viewing it rather from the point of view of the actual time of its definition as it admirably illustrates the long

[1] For these see pp. 120 ff.

wait which the Church often has before the guide speaks.

Now it needs to be emphasized that this is not some trifling issue. It has been, since 1854, a dogma of the Church which a man must receive on peril of eternal damnation. If, then, a man's eternal destiny is at stake, this is the time when the claim to have an infallible guide should be vindicated. But what in fact did happen? The battle was joined in earnest in the fourteenth century. Before that time, and subsequently, great names in the Roman Church are found in opposition to the idea – men like Bernard, Bonaventura, and Thomas Aquinas opposed it. The great protagonist on the other side was Duns Scotus. The Franciscans and the Dominicans were bitterly opposed to each other on the issue. The Council of Trent sat on the fence, though its decree on original sin seems to edge towards the views of the advocates of the new idea. But still the infallible guide remains silent, although the generations come and go; and the Church is left in doubt about a doctrine which subsequently proves necessary to salvation. At last, in the nineteenth century, when the storms of controversy had abated, and it was expedient to act, the Pope defined the dogma in the bull *Ineffabilis* (1854), and, astonishing as it may seem, he also decided that the Church had always held it!

The verdict of history is that the infallible guide waited nearly five centuries before he committed himself; and even the most lenient critic might be excused if he complains that this is an excessive delay. We may well ask whether the great advantages to the Church of an infallible guide are not somewhat overrated!

We turn to modern miracles and revelations; and here the problem is to select, for they are legion. From the many that have been accepted we will consider one which has been accepted and then, unfortunately for the adherents of the cult, denied. This is the case of the celebrated Philomena – a name familiar in many a Roman Catholic household where the practice of giving a saint's name to the child is common.

The development of the Philomena legend is typical of the reaction of Rome to such alleged modern revelations and miracles. At first they are tolerated as a popular devotion, and then, if the cult becomes widespread, it is officially endorsed and accepted. Such was the pathway to glory of Philomena before her sad eclipse.

The story in brief is that in 1802 a priest from Naples took home bones from Rome, which were then found to be the relics of one Philomena who was martyred in the persecution of the Emperor Diocletian. The foundation for this discovery was the dream of a nun in his congregation, who had a revelation of the facts of the life of Philomena and the miracles she performed. We might think that this was a rather dubious basis for accepting the story. In fact it is no more dubious than the alleged vision and revelation to the fourteen-year-old Bernadette at Lourdes, or the 'appearance' of the Virgin Mary to the children at La Salette, near Grenoble, in 1846, or Margaret Mary Alacoque's vision which was at first dismissed as delusion but later accepted and which led to the modern devotion to the sacred heart of Jesus. But dubious or not, the cult of Philomena grew. Leo XII proclaimed her a saint; Gregory XVI blessed one of her images; Pius IX – the Pope responsible for defining both the immaculate conception and papal infallibility – appointed an office and mass in her honour. The celebrated Curé d'Ars, who was canonized in 1928, lent the tremendous weight of his approval to the cult.

But then the bubble burst and Rome officially admitted there never was such a person as Philomena after all. Alas for those who have imagined that they bore the name of a holy virgin of the third century! But what about the more serious issue? With the full approbation of the Church, multitudes were permitted, or encouraged, to invoke her aid. Now it appears that they were simply invoking the figment of a nineteenth-century nun's imagination. Did the infallible guide know all along that the whole thing was completely baseless? If so, why did he not speak out? To let people engage in a so-called devotional exercise, which is superstitious and, in the event, also absurd, is surely to be culpable in the extreme – unless perhaps there is the excuse that the infallible guide did not know as much as the

77

fallible Dr Salmon who, nearly a hundred years ago, described Philomena as 'a being as imaginary as Desdemona or Ophelia'.[2]

But if we are surprised that the Pope was slow to act in the controversy over the Virgin Mary, if we are puzzled at his readiness to let the faithful embrace the most fanciful and baseless ideas, we will surely be astounded that in the most important dogma of all, from the Roman standpoint, namely his own infallibility, he should be so slow to act. Here for Rome is the foundation truth, since upon the assurance of having a divinely-appointed head she rests all her claims to authority, and so to the absolute submission of her people. Yet it was not until almost nineteen centuries of Christian history had passed that the Pope in 1870 defined his own infallibility.

The Roman Catholic will probably reply that this is a typical Protestant misrepresentation, and that the Pope in 1870 explicitly, formally, and so, infallibly, defined what had always been believed implicitly in the Church since the days of the apostles. We will deal later with the question as to what Scripture and the early Fathers have to say on the subject. Here we will deal only with the situation as it was in 1870, when the Pope promulgated the dogma.

There was a widely used catechism in Ireland called *Keenan's Catechism*, recommended by the Irish Roman Catholic hierarchy. According to Dr Ludwig Ott,[3] 'The Bishops exercise their infallible teaching power in an ordinary manner when they, in their dioceses, in moral unity with the Pope, unanimously promulgate the same teaching on faith and morals.' He adds, 'The agreement of the bishops in doctrine may be determined from the catechism issued by them.' Here, then, is a catechism with the imprimatur of the Scottish bishops, and the recommendation of the Irish bishops. There is no condemnation from Rome, so they had what Ott calls 'the tacit assent of the Pope'.

Now, one of the questions in this catechism was as follows: 'Must not Catholics believe the Pope in himself to be infallible?'

[2] *The Infallibility of the Church*, p. 198.
[3] *Fundamentals of Catholic Dogma*, p. 300.

The answer to this was, 'This is a Protestant invention: it is no article of the Catholic faith: no decision of his can oblige, under pain of heresy, unless it be received and enforced by the teaching body; that is, by the Bishops of the Church.' After 1870 this question and its answer were quietly dropped from the catechism. Now here we are not concerned with this dubious way of working, but with a more important issue. It is said that in 1870 the Pope made explicit what was already implicit in the faith of the Church; but it would take a great deal of verbal juggling to make the answer in the catechism an expression of the most rudimentary belief in papal infallibility. Furthermore, it would seem that Protestants prior to 1870 knew what the true teaching of the Roman Church really was, whereas the Irish and Scottish bishops did not.

In these different instances the Pope appears not as a leader giving clear guidance, but rather as an arbitrator who waits for the appropriate moment before trying to settle a dispute. But to be presented with an infallible guide who for long periods either cannot, or will not, or dare not speak on an issue of vital concern to the Church, is to be offered a very doubtful asset. It is no great advantage to have a pilot on board a ship who informs the captain only when he has safely entered harbour or when he has run on a sandbank. To pay a high price for a watch-dog, recommended as highly reliable, is to face a disappointment if we discover that the dog barks only after the intruder has been detected. It is easy to be wise after the event. But this kind of wisdom hardly qualifies for the designation infallible!

c. Infallibly Fallible

The Pope has not always been hesitant. There have been times when he has spoken out clearly and decisively, sometimes with favourable results, and sometimes with consequences that are disastrous for the Roman Catholic claim. One notable example of the former kind of pronouncement is that of Leo I, whose support of the orthodox position on the Person of Christ has often been quoted. Other illustrations could be given of papal support for the truth; and where such are produced we willingly accept them. It is no part of our case to belittle the orthodoxy of men like Leo. At the same time we cannot ignore other Popes who stand in marked contrast. In other words, our denial of papal infallibility is in no way affected by the orthodoxy, and the faithful testimony, of any number of Popes, whereas the Roman claim is completely overthrown if even one example can be adduced of a papal error. Unhappily for Rome the number of such errors over the centuries is considerable.

It may be well at the outset to counter in advance the reply which will probably be given. We shall be told that the Pope is infallible only when he acts in his official capacity as chief pastor of the Church. The Pope as a private theologian is quite fallible. It is only when his pronouncements are precisely defined and when they are *ex cathedra* that they are binding. While we may agree that it is hardly fair to condemn a Pope for some slip in general conversation, we must firmly maintain that if his pronouncement is apparently issued with his full authority, and if the Church at large accepts it as a true papal pronouncement, it seems a rather doubtful expedient to claim later that it was not such, because of some technical flaw in the manner of promulgation. We can imagine the public reaction to an authorized guide whose wrong directions have led some climbers to their death, and who then protests that the directions had not been written on the official notepaper!

One of the major heresies in the early Church was Arianism. In its denial of the true divinity of Christ it was obviously destructive of the gospel. The prime figure in the opposition to the heresy was not the Bishop of Rome, but Athanasius of Alexandria. Here surely was the chance for the infallible guide if such he was. But Pope Liberius unfortunately went sadly astray. He sided with the Arians, and excommunicated Athanasius. The latter indeed seemed to stand alone; but he battled on until he saw the truth vindicated. But what are we to say about papal infallibility in face of such a betrayal? Possibly the best reply to any attempts to justify Liberius is to quote the words of Hilary of Poitiers, the Athanasius of the West, and a canonized saint of the Roman Church. Here is one who was proclaimed a Doctor of the Church by Pius IX in 1851. His opinion of Liberius' judgment is aptly summed up in his devastating polemic, 'I say anathema to thee, Liberius, and to thy accomplices.'

The next century saw another battle. This time it was on another fundamental issue, namely the basis of our salvation. The contest was fought in North Africa where Pelagius and Celestius, with their virtual denial of the necessity of the grace of God, were opposed by the orthodox bishops led by Augustine. Again it was a situation where a visible head of the Church could have settled the dispute by an *ex cathedra* statement. Zosimus, the Pope, did act, but in the wrong way. He acquitted Pelagius and Celestius, and so endorsed their error in face of the African orthodox leaders. This was no hasty decision due to lack of information. It was delivered *Apostolicae sedis auctoritate* ('with the authority of the apostolic see'). Zosimus declares that he has not come to his decision 'hastily or untimely'. He pronounces that the two alleged heretics are impeccably orthodox (*absolutae fidei*). Later, under pressure, Zosimus withdrew; but the harm was done. The infallible guide had sadly blundered.

Pope Vigilius is one of those men with whom it is hard to sympathize. A man may make a serious mistake and then retract, and we can accept his withdrawal. But when a man adjusts his sails to every wind that blows, we find it difficult to have much respect for him. When such an example of vacillation and compromise is presented as the infallible, visible head of the Church, we are amazed at the distance we have moved from the apostle Paul whose yea and nay were so clear and unwavering. The Council of Chalcedon in AD 451 had declared the true doctrine of the Person of Christ as against the two heresies of Nestorianism and Monophysitism;[4] and it was on

[4] The Nestorians so emphasized the humanity of Christ that they virtually divided Him into two Persons, one human and one divine. The Monophysites, at the other extreme, so stressed His divinity at the expense of His humanity that in the one nature the human element was submerged.

81

this issue that the *Tome* of Leo had been a strong support for orthodoxy. But Vigilius was very different from Leo. He sided with the Monophysites in his *Judicatum*. As a result he was excommunicated by the African Church. He then switched his position backwards and forwards, and reached the position of endorsing the other heresy of Nestorianism. This was again no private opinion but a solemnly declared statement. He calls it a 'definition'. He writes 'we ordain and decree'. He stresses that this document, the *Constitutum*, is intended to be final. The Council meeting in Constantinople in AD 553, reckoned by the Roman Church to be the Fifth General Council, condemned Vigilius, who, true to form, gave way once again, and utterly repudiated his own former judgment. Here then was a situation where, far from being superior to a Council, the Pope was himself judged and condemned for heresy, and ultimately declared that his own solemnly defined judgments were in fact erroneous.

If we have scant sympathy for Vigilius we may have more for Honorius, for the heresy in which he was involved was a particularly subtle one – the 'monothelite' heresy, with its insistence on one will in Christ, as against the orthodox teaching that Christ had two wills corresponding to His two natures. He was condemned as a heretic by the Sixth General Council, and this condemnation was confirmed by Pope Leo II. Ludwig Ott maintains that he was wrongly condemned. But this does not save the Roman Catholic position. Whether he was personally orthodox or not, the Council obviously considered that a Pope might fall into heresy. Nor did this Council, any more than the one which condemned Vigilius, accept the modern Roman Catholic position that the Pope was above a Council. To them he was a bishop who was subject to their judgment, and in that judgment, endorsed by his successor, Honorius was adjudged heretical. Dr Ott argues that Leo condemned him only for negligence, not for heresy. How valid this excuse is may be discovered in Leo's own words when he anathematizes 'Honorius, who did not attempt to sanctify this Apostolic Church with the teaching of Apostolical tradition, but his profane treachery tried to subvert its spotless faith'. For centuries the condemnation of Honorius appeared in the Roman breviary, until it was removed in the sixteenth century. Once again we have a Pope in error, not in a private judgment, but in a statement made in his official capacity as head of the Church, for he solemnly 'defined' (the key word for Rome) his findings.

From the early centuries, when clearly Church Councils had no illusions about papal infallibility, we move on to a period when these claims were being made with increasing force. This time the Pope who blundered was Sixtus V (1585–1590), and the occasion of his wrong decision was his production of a standard version of the Vulgate. Anyone who has the slightest acquaintance with textual criticism will know that assessment of manuscripts is a matter for the expert. The amateur in this field is liable to make the most serious miscalculations. But Sixtus was a Pope who was sure of his own authority, and seemed to think that his official position conferred an ability to deal decisively with problems of textual criticism. So in 1590 his edition of the Vulgate appeared – the Latin Bible of the Roman Church.

Before we go on to consider the actual quality of this edition, it is best to deal with the possible reappearance of the old plea, that Sixtus was not acting and speaking *ex cathedra*. We quote his own words, prefaced to the edition. 'By the fulness of Apostolic power we decree and declare that this edition approved by the authority delivered to us by the Lord, is to be received and held as true, lawful, authentic and unquestioned, in all public and private discussion, reading, preaching and explanations.' Here is the kind of talk we expect from a man who claims to be an infallible guide. It is no wonder that he prohibits any change in this edition even of the smallest detail.

But not even the infallibility of Sixtus was enough for the scholars. It was obvious that he had made lots of mistakes. Indeed the work was patently the product of a novice. A new edition was called for and one where scholarship rather than infallibility should have the last word. In fact the scholars made about three thousand corrections! But how could this edition, produced in the time of Sixtus' successor Clement VIII, be introduced to the Church? Men could still recall the anathemas of Sixtus pronounced on any who dared to meddle with the product of his diligence. The solution to the problem which was adopted was to add a Preface in which the blame was laid on the printers! The author of this suggestion was a Jesuit, Cardinal Bellarmine. Certainly it was a way out, even if its ethics were deplorable. But it is really a poor attempt to cover up the indubitable fact that once again the infallible guide had gone sadly astray.

There remains the case of Galileo (1564–1642); but what an overwhelming indictment this was for the claims of the papacy. Here was the outstanding scientist of his day, who was condemned and silenced because he came into conflict with the Church. The significant fact is that the issue was ultimately theological, rather than scientific. The medieval scientists had maintained that the earth was the centre of the universe and the theologians had underwritten this with their interpretation of the Psalmist's words, 'Yea, the world is established; it shall never be moved.' [5] Galileo however came to see that the Copernican theory was correct, with its insistence that the sun was the centre around which the earth moved. As a believer in the truth of Scripture, Galileo was faced with a conflict between scientific fact, and what seemed to be biblical truth. His answer to this was that since Scripture could not err, it must be the interpretation of the Church that was at fault. So the conflict moved into the theological realm, for not only was Galileo questioning medieval astronomy, he was also questioning the pronouncements of the Church; and this was a much more serious affair.

The inevitable consequences followed. He faced the Inquisition, and was forced to accept their condemnation of his views. But he could not continue indefinitely in this position. He published a book called the *Dialogues*, in which the issue was discussed by two people. Galileo does not identify himself with either, but it was obvious where his sympathy lay. Indeed the Pope probably recognized in some of the arguments against the Copernican theory those which he had himself employed.

[5] Ps. 93 (92):1.

In any case he summoned Galileo to appear in Rome; and in spite of his age and illness – he was nearly seventy – he was compelled to appear. Here he was again condemned; and in face of the threat of torture, and possibly death, the old man capitulated and abjectly denied the truth of the theory which he knew to be true. Again it must be emphasized that the condemnation was not just on scientific grounds, but on theological. It was not the Pope acting as an amateur scientist who was involved, but the Pope acting in his capacity as the supreme guide of the Church in all matters of faith and morals.

It is all rather revolting, and indeed it is the kind of history which produces infidelity. But what is especially significant is that the chief actor in the whole brutal business was Pope Urban VIII. He it was who insisted that Galileo should come to Rome. It was in his presence that the inquisition declared its findings. It was to him personally that various appeals for leniency were made. And it was he who so persistently and cruelly tried to silence Galileo. His successors followed him, at least in their attitude, for the works of Galileo and Copernicus remained on the index of forbidden books until 1831 when, as Bishop Kerr said rather caustically, 'the earth received papal permission to move'.[6] For over two hundred years obscurantism reigned supreme, as the fixity of the earth was declared to be, not only a scientific fact, but the official view of the Catholic Church. Here surely is the supreme example of ignorant prejudice in face of clear scientific proof; and here too is the needle which pricks the pretentious bubble of papal infallibility.

[6] *A Handbook on the Papacy* (Marshall, Morgan & Scott, 1950), p. 253.

8

The sacraments

Roman Catholicism is essentially a sacramental religion. Thus God's grace, according to Catholic dogma, normally comes to men, not directly but mediately. Instead of the immediate contact which the Protestant claims to have with God in Christ, the Roman Catholic thinks rather of God coming to him through the sacramental ministry of the Church. 'Our sacraments both contain grace and confer it on those who receive them worthily.' [1] 'Since all the sacraments of the New Law were instituted by Christ our Lord as the principal means of our sanctification, the greatest care and respect must be paid to their profitable and proper ministry and reception.' [2]

For Rome there are seven sacraments, whereas the Protestant maintains that only in baptism and the Lord's Supper have we ordinances which Christ ordained, and to which He Himself attached an outward sign. Thus marriage, for example, is an ordinance of creation, and to say that Christ raised it to the level of a sacrament is to ignore two facts, one positive – that He simply recalled and re-emphasized the teaching of Genesis on marriage – and the other negative – that there is no outward sign ordained by Christ. Likewise in the case of confirmation and ordination there is no hint in the New Testament that the Lord has constituted them sacraments by means of some divinely given outward sign. Penance and extreme unction we will deal with later as these, we consider, are not biblical ordinances in any true sense at all. Küng's comments on the alleged sevenfold nature of the seven sacraments are apt. It is, he says,

[1] Karl Rahner (Ed.), *The Teaching of the Catholic Church* (Mercier Press, 1966), p. 258.   [2] *Ibid.*, p. 264.

'a product of history unknown during the first thousand years, presented for the first time in the twelfth century'.[3]

For the Roman Catholic his whole life from the cradle to the grave, and indeed beyond the grave in purgatory, is conditioned by this sacramental approach. We may summarize Rome's teaching on the seven sacraments thus: in baptism original sin is removed; in confirmation the Spirit is given; in the sacrament of penance mortal sins are forgiven; in the mass the priest offers on man's behalf the sacrifice by which sins are atoned for; in the hour of death he hopes for the unction to be administered by the priest. Should he be married or should he be ordained to the priesthood the grace required for either of these states of life comes again through the sacraments.

Closely allied to the stress on the sacraments is the stress on the priesthood, for apart from the case of baptism *in extremis*, the sacraments may be administered only by one who has been ordained to the priesthood by a bishop who is himself in communion with the Bishop of Rome, or, in the case of confirmation and ordination, by such a bishop.

According to the decrees of the Council of Trent, a sacrament is an effective sign of grace instituted by Christ. When we ask what precisely is the meaning, in this context, of the word 'effective' we are told by the creed of Pope Pius IV (II. 1. 8) that by divine institution a sacrament 'possesses the power both of effecting and signifying sanctity and righteousness'. In other words it is not simply a sign which declares a spiritual message, it actually effects something in the person to whom it is administered. So in the constitution on the sacred liturgy promulgated by Vatican II the assertion is made: 'From the liturgy therefore, and especially from the Eucharist, as from a fountain, grace is channelled into us' (I. 1. 10).

Thus sacraments are said to work *ex opere operato*; that is, by virtue of the performance of the act. The essentials of any sacrament are three: the matter, which is the physical substance used (or in the case of penance or marriage the action which can be perceived by the senses); the form, *i.e.* the word em-

[3] *Why Priests?* (Collins, 1972), p. 43.

87

ployed; and the minister with the right intention. Where these essentials are present there is, says Rome, a valid sacrament; and where there is such, grace is conveyed, not because of the faith of the recipient but by virtue of the sacramental act itself. It is true that Roman Catholic theologians have modified the rigidity of Trent and will insist on faith in the adult. But when we examine Trent on the subject we find that this faith is rather negative, for it is only in the sense of not placing an obstacle in the way of the grace of God that a man can be described as being in a right condition.

But this surely is to reduce the sacraments – even the two sacraments of the gospel which Protestants believe are the only ones entitled to that status, namely, baptism and the Lord's Supper – to the level of a magical incantation. The strong New Testament emphasis on the necessity of faith is hardly satisfied by the mere absence of a barrier. In the case of infants, and in the case of an unconscious man receiving extreme unction, there is no barrier. If then the 'sacraments' work *ex opere operato* we have here something completely apart from faith. Such a ceremony, while it may appear to belong to the New Testament, is really far removed from a religion in which the faith which is so strongly stressed is essentially an active laying hold of the promises of God, rather than a merely passive or negative condition.

Neuner and Dupuis point out [4] that the constitution on the sacred liturgy of Vatican II avoided the controversial phrase *ex opere operato* and emphasized rather the presence of Christ in the sacraments. But even if the phrase is not used and even though there is a stronger emphasis on faith, the underlying idea remains, if not so obviously in this decree, then certainly in the decree on the Church, and also in that on the priestly ministry and life. So the doctrine of baptismal regeneration is reaffirmed: 'The faithful . . . by baptism . . . are re-born as Sons of God. . . . In the family, human society's new citizens are born, whom baptism, by the power of the Holy Spirit makes into children of God.' [5] In other words, by birth you

[4] *The Christian Faith*, p. 360.   [5] Decree on the Church, II, xi.

become part of the human family, and by baptism you are made a child of God.

The sacraments however are nothing apart from the Word of God. Water, bread and wine have no significance until they are linked with the promises of the gospel. So they become declarations of the gospel. They are visible words declaring to the senses the same gospel which is proclaimed in the audible word of the preacher. But a word of promise requires not only the lack of any barrier; it requires the response of faith. To say that it does not is to treat the promise of God as of such little consequence that no positive reception of it is necessary. The reminder of Hebrews is a timely one: 'And without faith it is impossible to please him. For whoever would draw near to God must believe that he exists and that he rewards those who seek him.'[6] For Paul, writing to the Galatians, the hearing which is implied in the response of the Christian is essentially 'hearing with faith'.[7] Peter surely emphasizes the necessity of an inner change when he speaks of the cleansing of baptism as being 'not as a removal of dirt from the body but as an appeal to God for a clear conscience'.[8] Paul is equally emphatic that a religion which is acceptable to God is primarily and essentially inward. 'For neither circumcision counts for anything, nor un-circumcision, but a new creation.'[9] To claim that sacraments are more important than faith and to make them essential to salvation is to be confronted with the case of Simon Magus who was baptized, and who by Roman standards did not apparently place an obstacle, for he believed, though clearly only in the sense of assenting to the preaching (this however in Rome's view being sufficient!). Yet Simon is rejected by the apostle Peter in the strong words, 'you are in the gall of bitterness and in the bond of iniquity'.[1]

We have already mentioned a further important element in Roman Catholic sacramental teaching, namely the doctrine of intention. Without the right intention on the part of the priest there may be the correct matter (water, bread and wine); there

[6] Heb. 11:6.   [7] Gal. 3:2.   [8] 1 Pet. 3:21.
[9] Gal. 6:15.   [1] Acts 8:23.

may be the correct form (the Trinitarian formula, the words of institution); but there will not be a true sacrament. It is clearly therefore of great importance to know exactly what is meant by a right intention.

The Council of Trent in stressing the absolute necessity of the minister's intention also incidentally shows what is meant by the term. 'If any one saith, that in ministers, when they effect and confer the sacraments, there is not required the intention at least of doing what the Church does: let him be anathema.' Now this intention of doing what the Church does is not simply a matter of 'performing the external action with earnestness and in the proper circumstances',[2] for the inner religious significance must also be taken into consideration by the minister. Trent further stresses this fact, that intention means no mere external conformity, but an inner feeling, when it teaches on the 'sacrament' of penance that what is required is the 'intention on the part of the priest of acting seriously and absolving truly'. The same line is taken in the mass, for the words of institution in the Canon of the mass 'acquire consecratory power by the intention of the priest'.[3] So too in ordination the 'sacrament' is validly dispensed by the bishop 'provided he has the requisite intention',[4] though in this case a further intention is required on the part of the one who receives the Order. In a similar vein is the Roman rejection of Anglican orders in the bull of Pope Leo XIII, *Apostolicae Curae*, on the grounds that the Anglican ordinal is defective as far as any intention to confer sacerdotal powers is concerned.

But surely all this simply means that we can never be sure that a valid sacrament is being performed, and for any who accept the Roman Catholic view of the vital significance of the right use of the sacraments, such a position is spiritually disastrous. God alone knows the state of a man's heart. We can but look on the outward appearance and we may be completely deceived. After all Rome would freely admit that there have been many apostate priests, some of whom have lapsed into

[2] Ludwig Ott, *Fundamentals of Catholic Dogma*, p. 344.
[3] *Ibid.*, p. 393.   [4] *Ibid.*, p. 458.

complete infidelity. But clearly such a condition is not always reached overnight, and indeed a man might continue for a long time in that state without being detected. It is by no means unknown for a man to remain in an office which provides him with his living, while in his heart he has ceased to believe in the rites which he performs. Indeed it is quite possible that he may never be detected by men, and may die in a state of hypocrisy.

But how fares the doctrine of intention in such a situation? Such a man may not have performed a valid sacrament for years. What of all those who have been baptized by him? What of the masses which he has said on behalf of the faithful? And of even more solemn consequence to many an earnest soul, what of the value of the masses said for the departed in purgatory? What of those who have poured out their hearts in the confessional, and for whom the words of absolution have, unknown to them, been a mere hollow formula? The answer to all these agonizing questions comes, not from a Protestant propagandist, but from the great Cardinal Bellarmine: 'No one can be certain with the certainty of faith that he has a true sacrament, since the sacrament is not formed without the intention of the minister, and no one can see the intention of another.'[5]

The final impasse is reached when we discover that Rome permits baptism, *in extremis*, to be performed by someone other than a priest. The *Decretum pro Armenis* (1439) declares 'In case of necessity, however, not merely the priest or the deacon, but also a layman, even a woman, yea even a pagan or a heretic can baptize, provided he adheres to the form of the Church and has the intention of doing what the Church does.' But what guarantee is there that the heretic has the right intention? Indeed when I recall from personal knowledge the cynical attitude of some non-Roman Catholic medical students in Dublin who dutifully performed such a rite, it would seem that very few of such baptisms were valid.

Rome preaches salvation and links the way to heaven closely with the sacramental system. To the onlooker indeed this may

[5] Tom, 1, p. 488, prag. 1721.

appear as the great strength of such preaching. Surely here are objective realities on which you can fasten. But on closer examination the solid reality dissolves into uncertainty. The whole system becomes an unending series of questions. Are you sure you were baptized at all? Are you sure that the priest who officiated was validly ordained? What of the Pope himself? – can you be sure of every link in the chain which has led to his present position, that at every point the right intention was in the heart of each one who officiated at one of the sacraments? We are left grasping hopelessly at a vanishing image. Or perhaps better still, we are driven to see that the word of the gospel received directly by the heart of the faithful believer is the one ground of real assurance when all else is shifting sand.

9

The priesthood

It is quite apparent to the most casual onlooker that the Roman Catholic priest occupies a position completely different from that of the minister in one of the Reformed Churches. This is true not only of his status in Church dogma, but also of the attitude accorded to him by the laity. He is in a very real sense the key figure in the system, and inevitably so. A Church which is in its essential character sacramental will obviously pay particular attention to the person who performs the sacraments. But there is even more to it than that, for the priest not only acts as an official of the Church; he claims, rather, that he has, by virtue of his ordination, a special power enabling him to dispense to the faithful, by means of his sacramental ministry, the blessings of God.

The Council of Trent rejected the Reformers' teaching on the priesthood of all believers, and insisted that there is a special priestly state which is distinct from the lay condition. The admission to this state is itself sacramental, for it is by the 'sacrament' of ordination that a man is admitted to a position in the hierarchy. The material element in ordination is the laying on of hands; the form is the words of the bishop, with the formula appropriate to the particular orders being received – deacon, priest or bishop as the case may be; and as we have seen, the bishop who ordains must be in the so-called 'apostolic succession' and must have the right intention.

This ordination, it is claimed, confers a special grace on the recipient. Hence the document of Vatican II on the priestly ministry and life states that 'those ordained to the priesthood require, in addition to the basic sacraments which made them

Christians, a special sacrament through which, anointed by the Holy Spirit they are signed with a specific character and portray Christ the Priest and are thus able to act in the person of Christ our Head'.[1] As far as their ministry is concerned its focal point is the mass. 'The Eucharistic Assembly is the centre of the community of the faithful over which the priest presides. It is for the priests to teach the faithful to offer the divine Victim in the sacrifice of the Mass to God the Father.'[2] They are thus in a special way sharers in Christ's priesthood. As Pius XII expressed it in the *Mediator Dei*: 'the Sacrament of Order sets priests in a class apart from all other Christians who are not endowed with this supernatural power. They are made as it were, divine instruments to communicate the heavenly and supernatural life in the Mystical Body of Jesus Christ. . . . It is to the priests, then, that all must have recourse who want to live in Christ.'[3] The decree even goes so far as to claim that 'without priests the Church would be powerless to carry out her divine mission'.[4]

The Epistle which deals at length with this subject is that to the Hebrews. Here the great contrast is drawn between the old covenant and the new, and thus between the Levitical priesthood of the Old Testament and the priesthood of Christ. The Levitical priests were many in number and, as each generation passed, so a new group emerged to take their place. But by contrast, under the new covenant, there is but one great High Priest, the Lord Jesus Christ Himself, who, having offered the one final sacrifice for sins, is seated at the right hand of God. They were sinful, facing not only the sins of the people but their own. He is the spotless and sinless Son of God. Theirs was a glory which was passing; His the glory which surpasses and abides. He has offered once and for all the perfect sacrifice which has been accepted, and so through Him we may draw near to the throne of God.

Now it is of great significance that never in the New Testament is the ordained minister called a priest. The familiar word hierarchy, which means rule by priests, embodies the Greek

[1] I. 2.   [2] II. 5.   [3] III. 46–47.   [4] II. 11.

word for priest, *hiereus*. But this word is never once used in the New Testament for a Christian minister. He is called a 'presbyter' or elder, ordained to rule in the congregation and to minister the Word of God. He is called a 'bishop' or overseer, with the responsibility of pastoral oversight. But he is never designated a *hiereus*, for the conception of a sacrificing priestly caste is completely absent. It is perhaps of particular significance here that the apostle Peter, in referring to himself, does not use the title priest but writes, 'So I exhort the elders among you, as a fellow elder.' [5]

But the rejection of the idea of a priestly caste does not depend simply on the argument from silence. The apostle Paul could hardly be more emphatic than when he writes to Timothy 'For there is one God; and there is one mediator between God and men, the man Christ Jesus.' [6] Just as there is a uniqueness about the Godhead, and just as none dare usurp the prerogatives of God, for this would be blasphemy, so the Mediatorship of Christ is a unique one, and one therefore which cannot be shared.

What then of the distinction between priest and layman which the decree on the Church insists is an 'essential difference'? [7] This again vanishes in face of New Testament truth. The laity (Greek *laos*) embraces the whole people of God and does not refer to one section or group. Furthermore, the whole people of God are a nation of priests. The apostle Peter is not writing to the elders, but to the whole Church, as may be seen from the fact that in his Epistle there is an injunction for wives; and so it is the whole people of God which is described as 'a royal priesthood'.[8] So, too, the apostle John writing to the seven churches declares that Christ has made us 'a kingdom, priests to his God and Father'.[9]

The people of God are not priests in the sense of being able to offer a sacrifice to take away sins, for that one offering has already been made by the one High Priest. They are priests rather in the sense of having, in the words of Hebrews, 'con-

[5] 1 Pet. 5:1.　　[6] 1 Tim. 2:5.　　[7] 2:10.　　[8] 1 Pet. 2:9.
[9] Rev. 1:6.

fidence to enter the sanctuary by the blood of Jesus';[1] we can 'with confidence draw near to the throne of grace'.[2] They are priests in the sense of offering spiritual sacrifices. They offer 'the sacrifice of praise always to God, that is, the fruit of lips that acknowledge his name'.[3] There is the sacrificial offering of alms [4] and there is the offering of themselves when they hear the appeal of Paul to 'present your bodies as a living sacrifice, holy, and acceptable to God'.[5]

On this issue Hans Küng is refreshingly frank. He admits that 'all human priesthood has been fulfilled and finished by the unique, final, unrepeatable and hence unlimited sacrifice of the one continuing high priest'.[6] He acknowledges that 'the Church is constantly in danger of making itself and its organs into mediators'.[7] He is quite candid in his admission that the Lord's supper is 'the communal meal of the entire priestly people'. It is, he says, a later development which transformed it into 'a kind of new sacrifice offered by the leaders of the community on the community's behalf'. This he calls 'a misunderstanding which prepared the way for calling the leaders of the community priests and, as in pagan and Jewish tradition, distinguishing them from the rest of the people'.[8]

It is difficult to see how Küng squares his views with the decrees of Vatican II. The conservatives would, of course, contend that his teaching is completely subversive of the true Roman Catholic position. Certainly he is quite unequivocal in his rejection of the traditional Catholic view of the priesthood – a view which, as we have seen, is maintained by Vatican II. Thus he writes trenchantly of the pastoral ministry. Those in it 'are not at least as far as the New Testament tells us, a separate caste of consecrated priests, as they often are in primitive religions. They do not act as mediators between God and people by means of ritual actions which they alone can perform. . . . In the Church of Jesus Christ who is the only high

[1] Heb. 10:19.   [2] Heb. 4:16.   [3] Heb. 13:15.
[4] Heb. 13:16.   [5] Rom. 12:2.   [6] *The Church*, p. 366.
[7] *Ibid.*, p. 367.   [8] *Ibid.*, p. 382.

priest and mediator, all the faithful are priests and clergy.'[9] To all this we would add a hearty 'Amen'!

Küng has gone even further in his book *Why Priests?*[1] He demonstrates biblically that 'in contradistinction to the pagan or Jewish cult, a Christian does not need the mediation of a priest in order to enter the innermost sanctuary of his temple: that is, to reach God himself'.[2] He shows historically that the idea of a mediating priesthood was the product of the Middle Ages. It emerged from the fifth and sixth centuries as the ministry of the Word receded and 'cultic and ritual activity became that which was proper to the priesthood'.[3] It reached its climax late in the Middle Ages with the theory of the seven sacraments which he dates in the twelfth and thirteenth century. This theory demanded the appropriate sacerdotal office for the performance of the sacraments, and this it found in the developed view of the priesthood. This view, with its classic formulation in the Council of Trent, Küng emphatically rejects. He maintains that Vatican II moves somewhat from the Tridentine position but he still has to concede to the Council that 'from the dogmatic standpoint it maintained certain traditional structures of ministry'. A study of the documents of Vatican II will soon demonstrate that the maintenance of the structures is in fact emphatic and consistent.

Priestly activity, then, within the church is not the exclusive function of a special caste, but the ministry of the whole company of God's people. We are back to one of the basic tenets of the Protestant Reformation – the priesthood of all believers. Every believer has directness of access to God through the one mediator Christ Jesus. It is not through the Church, or through the priest, to Christ. It is rather directly through Christ to God the Father. Nor does the believer come to offer an atoning sacrifice; he comes rather on the basis of the offering already made by the High Priest, and he offers the sacrifices of praise and thanksgiving, and the sacrifice of his whole life. But he does this simply because he is a member of the people of

[9] *The Church*, p. 438.   [1] Collins, 1972.
[2] *Why Priests?*, p. 19   [3] *Ibid*., p. 38.

God in which every member is a priest. The man who is called to the ministry is indeed called to an honourable task. His commission, while it is recognized by the Church in the act of ordination, is ultimately from God.[4] The wisdom and spiritual gifts required for his task are from the Holy Spirit.[5] His is the ministry of feeding the flock.[6] He comes as an ambassador with the message of the King.[7] He points men to Christ. He warns; he rebukes, he exhorts; he encourages.[8] But he dare not trespass upon the unique ministry of the Saviour. It is not for him to intrude and to try and act as the sinner's advocate. It is for him rather to cry in the words of John the Baptist, 'Behold, the Lamb of God, who takes away the sin of the world!'[9]

[4] Acts 13:2; 2 Cor. 3:6. [5] Eph. 4:11.
[6] Jn. 21:15–17; Acts 20:28. [7] 2 Cor. 5:20.
[8] 2 Tim. 4:2. [9] Jn. 1:29.

10

Transubstantiation

The place of honour in the worship of the Roman Catholic is undoubtedly given to the mass.[1] While other services are optional this one is obligatory; and indeed it is a mortal sin to be absent without a sufficient reason. The whole conduct of the service emphasizes its importance. The priest wears special vestments which, through centuries of use, have been so identified with the mass that they become a visual declaration of the doctrine. The priest stands not at a table which would imply the family meal of the faithful, but at an altar which is essentially a place of sacrifice. The ringing of bells, the incense, the genuflections, all combine to stress that this is the supreme moment when the priest is believed to offer Christ as a sacrifice for the people of God.

But what the priest holds in his hand is bread and wine. How then does he claim to be offering Christ? The answer to this is the dogma of transubstantiation, which affirms that, through the priestly act of consecration, the substance of the bread and wine is changed into the body and blood of Christ so that what lies upon the altar is no longer bread and wine but Christ, and what the priest offers to God is nothing less than Christ Himself. Christ is the sacrificial victim, hence the designation of the bread as 'the host' (Latin *hostia*, 'victim').

This dogma, while its chief significance is in relation to the mass, also lies behind other popular forms of devotion. Because it is claimed that the presence of Christ is not limited to the

[1] The word 'mass' (Latin *missa*) is probably derived from the words of dismissal which closed the service in the Latin rite, *'ite missa est'*.

time of communion, but is a continuing reality, it is maintained that worship in its fullest sense may be offered to the consecrated host, since Christ Himself is being adored under the species of bread. The elaborate ritual on the feast of Corpus Christi, for example, when the consecrated host is borne in procession for the adoration of the faithful, is a particular manifestation of the dogma. So too, when the priest in the service of Benediction uses the consecrated wafer to bless the people, he would insist that it is the real presence of Christ, under the species of bread, which gives reality to the practice.

It is necessary to digress in order to meet the liberal protest that we are ignoring the liturgical movement in Rome. The old patterns are giving way to the new. Hans Küng for example dislikes the very term mass and prefers the Lord's Supper. This is not simply a matter of terminology but represents a new doctrinal emphasis. In view of this change, they would say that it is no longer relevant to discuss the traditional dogma of transubstantiation which was rooted in a medieval philosophy now abandoned by many modern Roman Catholic thinkers.

Our reply to this liberal objection is to refer them to the papal encyclical *Mysterium Fidei* in which, in face of the progressives' attempt to reinterpret transubstantiation, Pope Paul VI replied with a firm statement of the dogma, insisting not only on retaining the name of the dogma but also its essential meaning. He rejects the current idea of an omnipresence of the 'pneumatic' or spiritual nature of Christ's body in glory, and reiterates the traditional view which teaches what he calls the 'ontological reality', *i.e.* the essential reality of Christ's bodily presence. To complete the discomfiture of the progressives he finally endorsed the eucharistic cult with its veneration of the reserved sacrament – indeed he urged that this cult should be promoted; and if we ask the nature of this cult we have his reply that 'there has not been a time when she (*i.e.* the Church) has failed to venerate this great sacrament with the cult of worship which is due to God alone'.[2]

Paul VI continued this theme in his famous sermon, *Credo of*

2 Paragraph 55.

the people of God. In a firm reassertion of the traditional dogmas he turned to the mass. 'We believe', he declared, 'that the mysterious presence of the Lord (in the eucharist) is a true, real and substantial presence. Every theological explanation which seeks some understanding of this mystery must, in order to be in accord with Catholic faith, maintain that the bread and wine have ceased to exist after the consecration so that it is the adorable body and blood of the Lord Jesus.'

As we saw in the chapter on Catholic Pentecostalism the dogma still seems to be firmly entrenched there. The adoration of the reserved sacrament, so warmly endorsed in Thomas Flynn's book, is based squarely on the dogma. So too the charismatic movement's encouragement of devotion to the real presence, which elicited the approval of the American hierarchy.

It may be helpful at this point to sketch briefly the philosophical ideas underlying the dogma of transubstantiation. Take any body and you have, so it is taught, the 'accidents' which are available to your senses, that is sight, taste, smell, touch. But you also have the 'substance', or the underlying reality in which the accidents inhere. Thus if you have a piece of bread, it has a certain shape, a creamy colour, a softness, and a characteristic taste and smell. Here are the 'accidents'. But there is the essential quality which makes what you see, not just a collection of sense data, but an actual piece of bread, and this essential feature is the 'substance' of the bread.

Now, according to the dogma, after the words of consecration, the accidents remain but the substance is changed. Thus it still looks like bread, smells like it, tastes like it. But it has really only the appearance, for the substance has been changed into the body and blood of Christ. Thus the fifth article of the creed of Pope Pius IV maintains that 'in the most holy sacrament of the Eucharist, there are truly, really and substantially the body and blood together with the soul and divinity, of our Lord Jesus Christ; and that there is made a conversion of the whole substance of the bread into the body, and of the whole substance of the wine into the blood; which conversion the Catholic Church calls transubstantiation.'

But the dogma goes even further, for the creed adds, 'I also confess that under either kind alone (*i.e.* either bread or wine) Christ is received whole and entire.' Indeed, even when the bread is broken each particle is entire Christ. Thus Trent declares 'If any one shall deny that in the venerated sacrament of the Eucharist, entire Christ is contained in each kind, and in each several particle of either kind when separated – let him be accursed.' So every crumb of the wafer is entire Christ; every several drop of wine likewise.

A booklet for 'non-Catholic enquirers' gives us a popular version of the dogma. 'Catholics began to ask themselves the obvious question: what happens to the bread and wine when the words of consecration are pronounced? And the Church answered that the substance of the bread and wine simply ceased to exist, being replaced by the substance of Christ Himself, though the appearances (or qualities) of bread and wine remained to serve as a sort of envelope for the body of the Lord.' [3]

Now, like so many Roman dogmas, this one is a late addition to the apostolic faith. Its first formulation by a theologian did not appear until the ninth century when Paschasius Radbertus advanced the theory. He was resisted by Ratramnus of Corbey, and the debate continued until the final decision was taken at the Lateran Council in 1215. Duns Scotus, the great scholastic philosopher of the thirteenth century, and a Doctor of the Church, acknowledged that before this Lateran Council the dogma was not an article of faith. Certainly a thirteenth-century dogma could hardly be described as the doctrine of the early Church!

While our primary reason for rejecting the dogma is the testimony of Scripture, it may be of value to notice in passing how it also does despite even to common reason. Even granting, which many would not, the validity of the medieval conception of substance and accidents, we reach the position here that we have accidents without substance. The taste, colour, smell of

[3] E. R. Hull, S.J., *What the Catholic Church Is and What She Teaches* (Catholic Truth Society).

bread remain; but the substance of the bread has gone. But this is surely an absurdity. We are left with an Alice in Wonderland position where the Cheshire cat leaves its smile behind. Alice's exclamation 'a grin without a cat; it's the most curious thing I ever saw in my life' is an apt comment on this theory where the appearance of a thing remains while the reality has gone. If the bread is left and goes mouldy, is it the unsubstantial accidents which thus putrefy? If the reserved host should be eaten by a mouse, is the animal's appetite satisfied by the consumption of qualities from which the substance of bread has gone? And if it is maintained that Christ is now present, we ask where are the accidents of His body? They are there with His substance, we are told; but whereas His glorified body could be seen and touched by His disciples, now the accidents of that body have receded into the invisible realm, so that He is really present in bodily form, but neither substance nor accidents can be detected.

However it is the witness of Scripture, rather than philosophical juggling with words, which is the real answer to the dogma. We begin with the words of institution, 'This is my body . . . this is my blood.' Here, it is claimed, there is a clear and unambiguous statement by the Lord Himself, that the miracle has taken place; and so the bread is literally His body, and the wine is literally His blood. Hence the dogma may not have been formulated for centuries, but here it is implicitly stated.

We must insist, however, that this is figurative language. If Rome maintains that the statements are to be taken with an absolute and bald literalism, then she must be consistent and apply the same to other sayings of the Lord – 'I am the door'; 'I am the true vine'. Was He literally a door, literally a vine? Obviously this is absurd, and we readily recognize that He was using figures, or pictures, to describe His ministry. Again if we drive the baldly literal interpretation to its conclusion, we find ourselves in further difficulties with the Lord's statement at the Last Supper. 'This cup is the new covenant in my blood.' [4] Was

[4] 1 Cor. 11:25.

103

the substance of the literal cup changed so that only the accidents remained, and in its place there was the substance of the new testament? Again the reply is that this is absurd; but immediately we note that Paul introduces this statement of the Lord about the cup with the words, 'In the same way also the cup.' In other words he has just quoted the Lord's words concerning the bread, 'This is my body', and now, he continues, 'In the same manner, in a like fashion, he took the cup'. If, then, we reject as absurd the idea of a literal transubstantiation of the cup, must we not reject equally a crude literalism as applied to the earlier statements about His body?

It is important to study the Lord's words subsequent to His speaking the words of consecration. He has said 'This is my blood', and we are told that from that point onwards the wine was literally the blood of Christ. But immediately afterwards He refers to it quite clearly as still being wine. In fact the phrase He uses could hardly make it plainer that He regarded it as being in its natural state: 'I tell you I shall not drink again of this fruit of the vine until that day when I drink it new with you in my Father's kingdom.'[5] The apostle Paul writes in the same vein. Having described the institution of the supper, he explains the significance of eating and drinking. But again, it is as bread and wine that the elements are still described: 'For as often as you eat this bread and drink the cup, you proclaim the Lord's death until he comes.'[6]

Continuing with the original institution of the Lord's Supper we note that the Lord was Himself present in the flesh. Further, it was not the glorified humanity which He had after His resurrection, but the body of flesh and blood which He had received from His mother. Are we then to say that He, while there present in the integrity and unity of His humanity, also held His own body literally in His hands? Are we to say that, when the bread was broken into pieces, while He remained visibly and really before them, yet His body was now present in each particle?

If transubstantiation were a fact, then the eating and drinking

[5] Mt. 26:29; Lk. 22:18.   [6] 1 Cor. 11:26.

104

would be a literal partaking, and not a spiritual feasting by faith. But how would this square with the decree of the Council of Jerusalem which commanded an abstinence from blood? [7] Furthermore it would mean that the wicked would actually eat the body and drink the blood of Christ. But Christ Himself says of all those who eat that they will live for ever; that they have eternal life; and that He will raise them up at the last day.[8] Clearly these promises can apply only to those who truly partake of Christ, and while the wicked may eat the bread and drink the wine they do not receive Christ Himself.

Indeed, far from John 6 being capable of a literalistic interpretation, the Lord Himself rejects such in the very same discourse. The disciples found His words hard, for they obviously took them in a literal way. Hence the significance of Christ's reply, 'It is the spirit that gives life, the flesh is of no avail. The words that I have spoken to you are spirit and life.' [9] That is to say, to receive His body would not avail for the salvation of their souls, and they must therefore realize that these words have a spiritual meaning. It follows that to interpret His words in a grossly literal fashion is to miss the whole point of His teaching; for He is speaking of a spiritual eating and drinking. It is eating and drinking by faith that is in view. A clear confirmation of this comes earlier in the chapter. 'He who comes to me shall not hunger and he who believes in me shall never thirst.' [1] To eat and drink is to come to Christ, to have faith in Him, and so to share in the results of His death.

An interesting comment on all this comes from the great Doctor of the Church, Augustine of Hippo, in the fourth century, where he gives guidance for determining whether a passage is to be taken literally or figuratively. 'If a passage is preceptive, and either forbids a crime or wickedness or enjoins usefulness or charity, it is not figurative. But if it seems to command a crime or wickedness, or to forbid usefulness or kindness, it is figurative. "Unless you eat", He says, "the flesh of the Son of Man, and drink His blood, you have no life in you." He appears

[7] Acts 15:29.   [8] Jn. 6:51–55.   [9] Jn. 6:63.
[1] Jn. 6:35.

to enjoin wickedness, or a crime. It is a figure, therefore, teaching us that we partake of the benefits of the Lord's passion, and that we must sweetly and profitably treasure up in our memories that His flesh was crucified and wounded for us.' [2]

The objection will be raised that if, in fact, the wicked do not receive the body and blood of Christ, what is the point of the apostle Paul's solemn warning? The answer to this is an examination of what Paul actually says. He writes: 'Whoever, therefore, eats the bread or drinks the cup of the Lord in an unworthy manner will be guilty of profaning the body and blood of the Lord.' [3] Now it is significant that what the wicked are described as receiving is not the body and blood, but the bread and the cup. Their guilt was that they had received the Lord's own divinely given sign, and yet had rejected the Lord Himself. In the days of His earthly ministry Christ had the sternest rebuke for those who heard His word with their outward ears but did not receive it by faith with their hearts. So here; Paul is speaking about the visible word of the sacrament in which Christ is preached by the ordinance which He has ordained. How serious it is, he says, to receive this visible word and yet to refuse the One to whom the word bears witness.

But the objector continues: What then of Paul's further charge that their guilt lay in the fact that they were 'not discerning the body of the Lord'? [4] Was it not because they did not discern the Lord's real presence in the sacrament that they acted unworthily? But we reply that not even the most ardent advocate of transubstantiation can recognize the Lord's body in any literal sense, for on his own confession neither substance nor accidents are present to the senses. To 'discern the Lord's body' in the sacrament is to see by faith the inner meaning and spiritual significance of the elements of bread and wine. When Paul writes to the Galatians, and recalls that before them 'Jesus Christ was publicly portrayed as crucified',[5] he did not mean that they had actually seen Jesus crucified. He meant that in

[2] *The Third Book upon Christian Doctrine* (Benedictine Edition, 1685), III, p. 52.
[3] 1 Cor. 11:27.   [4] 1 Cor. 11:29.   [5] Gal. 3:1.

the preaching of the gospel they had by faith seen Christ crucified. So to discern or recognize the Lord's body in the sacrament
is to see by faith Christ crucified set forth before us. Bread and
wine set forth the gospel of Christ crucified, and to receive the
gospel means an attitude of repentance and faith. But these
Corinthians were in a very different frame of mind. Their sin
was indeed primarily their lack of consideration for the other
members of the Church. Thus gluttony and selfishness are the
sins which are rebuked here; and it was the presence of these
that made their reception of the bread and wine so serious a
matter. But we must emphasize again that, for the apostle,
what they are eating and drinking is the bread and the cup, and
not the actual body and blood of the Lord.

The dogma of transubstantiation ignores the New Testament
doctrine of the ascension. The Lord visibly, on the Mount of
Olives, ascended before His disciples. We say in the Nicene
Creed, 'He ascended into heaven and sitteth on the right hand
of God the Father Almighty'. The Epistle to the Hebrews
emphasizes this heavenly reign of Christ. He is at the right hand
of the majesty on high. Now this ascended Lord is the One who
with the Father sends to His people the Holy Spirit 'who
proceedeth from the Father and the Son'. This is in accordance
with His promise to His disciples that He would not leave them
'desolate' (literally 'orphans').[6] So he speaks words of comfort.
He is going away but He will come again. And how will He
come? In His bodily presence in the sacrament? No! He comes
now through His Spirit, and at the last day He will come again
as visibly and openly as He ascended.[7]

Now Paul takes this fact of the absent Christ, whose coming
again at the end of the age is the constant hope of the Church,
and links it with his sacramental teaching. In the communion,
he says, we show forth the Lord's death 'until he comes'.[8] Every
time we meet at the Lord's table, we declare to one another
that the Lord has not yet come; and in our communion we look
forward to that coming. True we have not been left as orphans,
for we believe and know that He is present with us by His Holy

[6] Jn. 14:18.   [7] Acts 1:11.   [8] 1 Cor. 11:26.

107

Spirit. But His bodily coming is as yet in the future, and so we pray, 'Come, Lord Jesus'.[9] But if in fact He comes in bodily fashion as the substance of bread and wine give way to His, then surely it would be folly to look forward to His coming as yet in the future. Yet Paul insists that we do thus look forward. Our absent Lord will soon appear and we press on towards that glad day. But such a hope completely excludes an alleged bodily presence already here. When He comes it will not be with a 'substance and accidents' hidden from view, but, according to the promise, it will be in like manner as the disciples saw Him go.

The dogma of transubstantiation, rationally and scripturally untenable, has had disastrous consequences. We have seen some of these already in the practice of the adoration of the consecrated host. It is a far cry from the plain command 'Take and eat this' to the worship of a Corpus Christi procession. But there is another serious consequence which largely stems from the dogma, namely the withholding of the cup from the laity. The plea made for this is the possibility of spilling the wine which would, if the dogma were true, be too terrible to contemplate. To meet the objection that the communicant is being denied a vital part of the sacrament, the dogma is again invoked to support the claim that to receive the bread is sufficient, for Christ is completely present under either species.

Now like the dogma itself, this withholding of the cup from the laity was a late development which was only finally formulated at the Council of Constance in 1415. Certainly the cup was not withheld in the early Church, and quite emphatically it may be asserted that it was not withheld in the New Testament period. When the Lord instituted the communion He said quite plainly as He handed them the cup 'Drink of it, all of you'.[1] So, too, when Mark is describing the scene he is equally clear: 'they *all* drank of it'.[2] In the apostle Paul's discussion of the subject in 1 Corinthians 11 his constant references to the receiving of the cup show that this was the normal practice.

A significant comment on the practice of the early Church is

[9] Rev. 22:20.   [1] Mt. 26:27.   [2] Mk. 14:23.

found in the words of Chrysostom, writing as late as the fourth century. He emphasizes that there is no distinction between minister and people in the communion. 'Whereas under the old Covenant the priests ate some things and the laymen others; and it was not lawful for the people to partake of those things of which the priest partook; it is not so now, but one body is placed before all, and one cup.'[3]

What is sorely needed is a return to the simplicity of the upper room. To see the Lord setting apart the bread and wine as the tokens of His approaching death; to see the disciples receiving, and eating and drinking by faith; to hear the call to continue this in the life of the Church – all this is to move in an atmosphere far removed from the philosophical speculations of transubstantiation and from the sad consequences which have flowed from that dogma.

[3] Homily XIV on 1 Corinthians.

11

The mass

The mass is said to be both a sacrament and a sacrifice. It is a sacrament in so far as the worshipper is nourished by the body and blood of Christ. But it is also a sacrifice in that it is a gift offered to God. In the mass considered as a sacrament Christ is received by the faithful. In the mass considered as a sacrifice Christ is offered by the priest, on behalf of the people, to God the Father.

Now Rome is at pains to stress that the mass is not a separate or independent sacrifice. It does not stand over against Calvary as being an additional sacrifice. Indeed, it is claimed that it is the same sacrifice, only offered in a different way. 'The mass is the same sacrifice as that of the cross, because in both we have the same victim and the same offerer; for the same Christ, who once offered Himself a bleeding victim to His Heavenly Father on the cross, continues to offer Himself in an unbloody manner, by the hands of His priests on our altars.' [1]

Thus the mass may be viewed as the means by which the sacrifice of Calvary is made present. It is thus defined by the Roman Catechism as a 'renewal' of the sacrifice of the cross. But this must not be misunderstood as teaching that it is only a commemoration or a dramatic re-enactment. It is in itself, because of its relation to Calvary, a real sacrifice.

One means of commending this teaching to the hesitant non-Roman Catholic is the invocation of the idea of the eternal self-offering of Christ. Thus it is said that Christ's offering is not one which can be tied to time, but is being eternally offered. Hence it is claimed that, when the priest offers the mass, he is simply united to Christ in His self-offering. Thus E. R. Hull

[1] *Catechism of the Synod of Maynooth*, p. 51.

writes: 'Christ's offering of Himself, which began when He came into the world, continues for ever in Heaven. Hence when at the consecration of the Mass He comes down to the earthly altar, He is still offering Himself, an eternal victim all the time.' [2]

But obviously we must ask further what kind of sacrifice does the mass represent? In the New Testament, sacrificial language is freely employed – we offer our bodies as a sacrifice; [3] we offer alms; we offer the sacrifice of praise and thanksgiving.[4] Does the mass come into this category? The decrees of Trent are quite clear that it does not. It is not only a sacrifice of praise and thanksgiving but is also, to use terms which will require further explanation, a propitiatory and impetratory sacrifice.

A 'propitiation' is an offering made to God in view of His offended justice. The sinner's rebellion is an affront to God's holiness, and therefore calls forth God's condemnation. But the propitiation is that which God provides, whereby He becomes propitious, or favourable, to the sinner. Hence the mass as a propitiation is offered to effect the remission of sins. It is claimed further that this propitiation avails not only for the living, but for the faithful departed in purgatory who can 'be helped above all by the sacrifice of the altar which is pleasing to God'.

An 'impetratory' sacrifice is one that makes an appeal to God. Hence it is a powerful form of intercession for the procuring from God of natural blessings, and also supernatural graces. One can therefore understand the saying of a mass with a particular intention, that is with a desire or request presented to God for some specific need. Thus, while the mass is in Trent's teaching a propitiatory sacrifice 'for sins, for punishment for sins, and for expiations', it is also an impetratory sacrifice, that is a sacrifice of appeal, 'for other necessities'.

As far as the guilt of sin and the temporal consequences of sin are concerned, the sacrifice of the mass is said to operate in

[2] *What the Catholic Church Is and What She Teaches*, p. 31.
[3] Rom. 12:1.   [4] Heb. 13: 15, 16.

different ways. In the matter of guilt it does not act directly but mediately, by obtaining the grace of repentance. 'Propitiated by the offering of this sacrifice, God, by granting the grace and gift of penance, remits trespasses and sins, however grievous they may be.' When we turn to the consequences of sin, however, whether those in this life or those endured in purgatory, the effect of the mass is claimed to be direct or immediate, for the sacrifice is offered in lieu of the good works which, Rome would teach, must be offered as an atonement for previous wrongdoing, and as a substitute for the sufferings of those in purgatory.[5]

The mass, then, is not simply the eucharist, or thanksgiving, of the faithful. It is the supreme moment in the Church's worship when the priest claims to offer Christ as a sacrifice for the living and the dead. Behind it, of course, lies the dogma of transubstantiation which we have already considered. It is because of the alleged change of the substance of the bread and wine into the body and blood of Christ that the sacrifice is possible. Thus the wafer is no longer bread, but the consecrated host – and it is therefore the divine victim who is offered by the priest each time mass is said.

Pope Pius XII in his encyclical *Mediator Dei* reaffirmed the teaching of the Council of Trent. He wrote: 'The august Sacrifice of the Mass is therefore no mere commemoration of the Passion and Death of Jesus Christ, it is truly and properly the offering of a sacrifice wherein by an unbloody immolation the High Priest does what He had already done on the Cross, offering Himself to the Eternal Father as a most acceptable victim.'[6] As he held this view of the mass Pius XII did not consider communion, in the sense of receiving the elements, to be necessary for the faithful. 'While it (*i.e.* reception of the sacrament) is quite necessary for the sacrificing minister, to the faithful it is only to be highly recommended.'[7]

The same basic conception of the mass as a sacrifice continues in the documents of Vatican II. The constitution on the

[5] See chapter 14 for discussion of works of satisfaction.
[6] Part 2, I. 72.   [7] Part 2, III. 122.

sacred liturgy certainly took great strides in encouraging con-
gregational participation, but it still maintains the position of
Trent: 'One . . . and the same is the victim, one and the same
is He Who now offers by the ministry of His priests, and Who
then offered Himself on the Cross; the difference is only in the
manner of offering.' [8] So for Vatican II the 'eucharistic sacrifice'
was instituted 'to perpetuate the sacrifice of the cross throughout the centuries'.[9] Hence the Church building is especially
sacred, for 'Here is present the Son of God, our Saviour,
offered for us on the altar of sacrifice.' [1] It is an echo of Pius
XII when he spoke of the priestly function: 'The priest places
the divine victim on the altar. He presents it as an oblation to
God the Father for the glory of the Blessed Trinity and for the
benefit of the whole Church.'

In the encyclical *Mysterium Fidei* Pope Paul VI asserted
even more insistently (and indeed in face of the progressives,
with passion) that the traditional view of the eucharistic sacrifice must not only be maintained and defended but taught and
encouraged. This encyclical was issued just before the fourth
session of the council and marked not only a rebuff to the
progressives but, even more significantly, a strongly-worded
check to the whole movement of thought which had already
been expressed in the Constitution on the Sacred Liturgy
(promulgated on 4 December 1963, in the first document published by Vatican II). Now this constitution had applied
some of the liturgical principles which the progressives have so
strongly advocated – and of which, incidentally, we have all
heard so much. In it there was a swing in emphasis from the
conception of the private mass to that of the mass in which the
communicants take a more active part, 'knowingly, actively and
fruitfully'.[2] With this in view the vernacular was introduced,
the sermon was given a new prominence, more readings from
Scripture were ordered, the calendar of the Church's year was
scheduled for revision in order that prominence would be given

[8] Council of Trent, Twenty-second Session, II.
[9] Constitution, ch. 2 : 47.
[1] Decree on the Priestly Ministry and Life, II. 5.   [2] I. 13.

to the Lord's Day and to the events which commemorate the saving acts of Christ, and, an even more striking innovation, the first steps were taken towards restoring the cup to the laity. It is no wonder that the progressives felt that the tide was flowing their way. The new road seemed to be leading away from the solitary mass to what they were now calling the Lord's Supper.

So the constitution decreed, 'It is to be stressed that whenever rites, according to their specific nature make provision for communal celebration involving the presence and active participation of the faithful, this way of celebrating them is to be preferred, as far as possible to a celebration that is individual and quasi-private. This rule applies with special force to the celebration of Mass and the administration of the sacraments even though every Mass has of itself a public and social nature.'[3] In other words, the social conception of the mass was made the norm and the private mass was merely the exception which was still allowed.

But the Pope completely reversed this pattern with his encyclical. He voiced his anxiety that the opinions being propagated were liable to disturb the minds of the faithful: 'Such opinions', he said, 'relate to Masses celebrated privately, to the dogma of transubstantiation and to eucharistic worship.' And on these three issues he took a line diametrically opposed both to the progressives and to the concessions in the decree already issued. He reminded them that they must not imagine 'that although a doctrine has been defined once by the Church, it is open to anyone to ignore it or to give it an interpretation that whittles away the natural meaning of the words or the accepted sense of the concepts.'[4]

Then follows an uncompromising statement of the traditional teaching. The Council of Trent's formulation is endorsed and any modification of Tridentine formulae is declared to be intolerable. The old doctrine of the mass is emphasized, together with the doctrine of purgatory: 'Instructed by the Lord and the Apostles, the Church has always offered it not only for

[3] I. 27.   [4] Paragraph 10.

the sins, punishments, satisfactions and needs of the faithful still alive, but also for those who have died in Christ but are not yet fully cleansed.'[5] Then again the introduction into the constitution of the idea of the priesthood of all believers met a firm rejoinder in the Pope's insistence that a distinction between the priesthood of the faithful and the hierarchical priesthood 'is not a distinction of degree alone but of essence'.[6]

By way of reply to all this we begin with the institution of the communion at the Last Supper and at once we can see that any attempt to give a sacrificial meaning to the command of the Lord, 'Do this', founders on the rock of the context of the words. In no sense can they be made to mean 'offer this sacrifice', for in actual fact they are explained quite clearly in terms of eating and drinking. Speaking of the cup the Lord says 'Do this, as often as you drink it, in remembrance of me.'[7] And Paul adds the comment that in this service the believers thus show forth the Lord's death 'as often as you eat this bread and drink the cup'.[8] 'Do this' simply means eat and drink; and indeed it is a sad comment on the straits to which the exigencies of controversy drive men that it is necessary to stress what would seem to be such an obvious truth.

We ask further – in view of the fact that the Last Supper is claimed as the first mass – did Christ then offer Himself to the Father? Surely His sacrifice was still in the future. The broken bread and the outpoured wine were as yet prophetic, for they looked forward to an event yet to come just as now they look back to an event that has taken place. Indeed the Lord Himself drew this distinction between the Supper, and the suffering which lay beyond it: 'I have earnestly desired to eat this passover with you before I suffer.'[9] One might therefore as readily claim that the Lord was offering His sacrifice when earlier it is said that 'he set his face to go to Jerusalem',[1] for at that point we see the clear and determined purpose which led Him to Calvary. But these words and acts were not the offering, for the apostle John can repeat again and again the words 'His hour

[5] Paragraph 29.   [6] Paragraph 31.   [7] 1 Cor. 11:25.
[8] 1 Cor. 11:26.   [9] Lk. 22:15.   [1] Lk. 9:51.

had not yet come'. While the Lord may foretell His passion by the words He speaks, and by the institution of the Supper, yet the sacrifice itself belongs to 'the hour', the decisive hour determined by the Father. Not until then can we speak of the sacrifice as accomplished.

Continuing our examination of the Last Supper, it is of the utmost importance to notice that there is no hint of an offering being made to God, for in fact the offering is made rather to men. The Lord is addressing the disciples and not His Father. It is to them He gives the bread and the cup. It is to them He declares the meaning of the bread and the wine. It is to them that He gives the command to take and eat, to take and drink. The whole emphasis is on their reception of His gifts rather than on any thought of an offering by them of a sacrifice to the Father.

This is confirmed by the word which the apostle Paul uses in describing the mutual encouragement and blessing which comes through the sharing together of the bread and wine by the people of God – 'For as often as you eat this bread and drink the cup, you proclaim the Lord's death until he comes.' [2] The significant word here is that translated 'proclaim' which Knox well translates 'heralding'. The verb [3] is used seventeen times in the Acts of the Apostles and in the writings of the apostle Paul to describe the preaching of the gospel. But such preaching is obviously directed to men. We pray to God; we offer praise to God; but we preach to men. So then, when Paul speaks here of heralding the Lord's death, he is not suggesting a spreading forth of the sacrifice before God, but is rather describing the declaration of the gospel to the worshipper. As we each one take the bread and the wine, we declare to those who are meeting with us the gospel of a crucified Christ. The bread and the wine are not only the 'visible word' by which God speaks His word of mercy to us individually. Here is also the word which we, by our participation in this service, declare to our fellows. Thus the service is not only one of communion with the Lord but of communion with each other.

[2] 1 Cor. 11:26.   [3] Greek *kataggellō*.

116

We turn to the Epistle to the Hebrews which, possibly more than any other book in the New Testament, sounds what should be the death knell of the whole conception of the mass as a sacrifice. Here the dominant theme is the finality of the revelation which God has made in Christ. God has indeed spoken His Word through the Old Testament writers; but here is His final Word. God has spoken through Christ in such a way that there is no further Word to add, and all that is now required is an understanding of that Word, and a humble and obedient acceptance of it.

Now the finality of Christ's revelation relates especially to His death on our behalf. Here the language and the imagery are especially vivid. Christ is pictured as having done His work, and having sat down at the right hand of the Father.[4] To sit down after a task is to indicate the completion of the task. Here then is One who has finished His work, and who, by the very place of honour which He occupies, declares that His offering has been already accepted. The picture then is not of some priest before the throne offering a sacrifice. There is no hint of Christ's eternal self-offering. Instead the vision is of One who sits on the throne, and awaits the final consummation of His Father's purposes, when His enemies shall become His footstool. When He intercedes for His people it is not as One presenting His sacrifice, but as One whose sacrifice has already been presented and accepted.

This finality of the sacrifice of Christ, which so conflicts with the conception of the 'renewal' of that sacrifice in the mass, is further emphasized by the contrast between the sacrifice of the Old Testament and that of Christ. Here the significant words appear again and again – 'once', 'once for all' – to emphasize the perfection and the finality of Christ's offering. Thus we read, 'he entered once for all into the Holy Place, taking not the blood of goats and calves but his own blood, thus securing an eternal redemption'.[5] Now this 'once for all' entry is by contrast with the repeated offerings of the Levitical priests. So we read further, and what a devastating reply it is to the idea of the

[4] Heb. 1:3; 8:1; 10:12f.; 12:2.   [5] Heb. 9:12.

constant priestly offering of the mass – 'Nor was it to offer himself repeatedly, as the high priest enters the Holy Place yearly with blood not his own; for then he would have had to suffer repeatedly since the foundation of the world. But as it is, he has appeared once for all at the end of the age to put away sin by the sacrifice of himself.'[6]

Nor are we left wondering as to the precise significance of the repeated word 'once' or 'once for all'. The analogy is drawn from death, which is in a unique sense a 'once for all' experience, and one that is in no sense repeated or renewed or re-enacted. It happens once and only once. So comes the application of the analogy, with its further indictment of the doctrine of the mass. 'And just as it is appointed for men to die once, and after that comes judgment, so Christ, having been offered once to bear the sins of many, will appear a second time, not to deal with sin but to save those who are eagerly waiting for him.'[7]

But there is a further word to stress the truth, that there is no need to repeat this sacrifice, whose sufficiency has already been declared by God. Of the Levitical priests it is said, 'every priest stands daily at his service, offering repeatedly the same sacrifices, which can never take away sins'.[8] In other words the very repetition of the sacrifices shows their insufficiency. Indeed earlier this very point was made. If the sacrifices had been sufficient 'would they not have ceased to be offered'?[9] The daily offering is a comment on their imperfection, and is a comment too on the perfection of Christ's single offering. 'But when Christ had offered for all time a single sacrifice for sins, he sat down at the right hand of God. . . . For by a single offering he has perfected for all time those who are sanctified.'[1]

Hebrews of course does not stand alone in this testimony to the finished work of Christ. In fact this truth is the very foundation of the whole New Testament teaching on the way of salvation. The apostle Peter, for example, uses one of the characteristic words of Hebrews when he speaks of Christ's

[6] Heb. 9:25f.   [7] Heb. 9:27f.   [8] Heb. 10:11.
[9] Heb. 10:2.   [1] Heb. 10:12, 14.

118

death being a ransom paid 'once for all'.[2] So too in Romans the apostle Paul uses the other Greek word of Hebrews to speak of Christ's death as being 'once for all'.[3] On this verse Knox's explanatory footnote is a telling comment. 'Christ died to sin, in the sense that the burden of human sins which He freely took upon Himself demanded, as of right, His death, but now, having undergone that sentence, He has satisfied all the obligations which His condescension brought upon Him.'

Any service, therefore, which purports to renew the sacrifice of Calvary is a plain denial of the overwhelming testimony of Scripture to the perfection of the Lord's one offering. The doctrine of the mass implies the imperfection and insufficiency of the sacrifice of Calvary, for the latter needs now to be supplemented by the daily offering at the altars of the Church of Rome. But what need is there of any attempt to present a sacrifice to God? The Lord has already presented it and has been accepted. The ransom has been paid, and that payment is no mere event of past history for, says Hebrews, 'the ransom he has won lasts for ever'.[4] Let our blessed Lord speak the last word on this whole matter of the completeness, finality, and once-for-all character of His sacrifice. That word comes in the shout of triumph which rang out from His lips in His closing moments on the cross, 'It is finished'.[5] Such a consummation, accomplished by the great High Priest Himself, leaves no place for the sacrifice of the mass.

[2] 1 Pet. 3:18.   [3] Rom. 6:10.   [4] Heb. 9:12 (Knox).
[5] Jn. 19:30.

119

12

Ave Maria

We begin with a word of whole-hearted agreement with Rome as she acknowledges the truth of the virgin birth. When we hear Roman Catholic thinkers vigorously repudiate the liberal position that the virgin birth is not strictly true from a historical standpoint, but simply conveys an important religious truth, we are ready to endorse their protest heartily. Like them, when we confess in the Apostles' Creed that Christ was 'born of the Virgin Mary', we are declaring our faith in the unique event of the incarnation when Mary bore a child, conceived not by means of a human father, but by the operation of the Holy Spirit.

We are not so ready, however, to follow Rome when she takes the next step and claims that Mary, after the birth of the Lord, continued a virgin. The 'perpetual virginity' of Mary may well be a topic for debate in which different conclusions may be drawn, but, most emphatically, it can never be a subject for dogmatic assertion. Indeed the form of the language of Matthew 1:25 seems to weigh heavily against it. Knox in his attempt to safeguard the dogma perpetrates what, with all the fairness it is possible to muster, we can only describe as a grievous mistranslation. Once again, however, he redeems the situation by giving a literal rendering in his footnote. Thus, after the mistranslation, 'he (*i.e.* Joseph) had not known her when she bore a son, her first-born', he adds the literal rendering, 'he knew her not till she bore a son'. But surely the plain and obvious meaning of the language, if one were not trying to establish some theory, is that, after the miraculous birth, Joseph and Mary came together as husband and wife in the fullest sense.

The fact that Jesus is described as her first-born obviously does not of itself mean that there were other children. But when we find later that Mary is accompanied by those who are called the brethren of the Lord, it seems again most natural to take the title 'first-born' as being literally true. If we take the biblical view of marriage in which the physical union is divinely ordained, then we will see nothing strange in the fact that Mary should thus be united with Joseph and bear children. Indeed if the apostle Paul could view the 'one flesh' relationship of marriage as being a picture of the union between Christ and His Church, then the union of Joseph and Mary in a fully consummated marriage becomes perfectly understandable. It is a rather lame reply to all this to argue from Mary's query to the angelic messenger, 'How can this be, since I have no husband?',[1] that she had made a vow of perpetual virginity. For a young woman facing a perplexing problem it was an obvious question to ask. Those who find here such an underlying vow to a permanent state of virginity are reading far too much into it.

There are however much more serious grounds for disagreement, when we find Rome making even more far-reaching claims for Mary. The year 1854, with its promulgation by Pope Pius IX of the dogma of the Immaculate Conception, marked the end of a debate which had gone on for centuries. This new dogma, from that point to be believed by all the faithful, stated: 'The Most Holy Virgin Mary was, in the first moment of her conception, by a unique gift of grace and privilege of Almighty God, in view of the merits of Jesus Christ the Redeemer of mankind, preserved free from all stain of original sin.'

Ludwig Ott is refreshingly frank when he admits that the doctrine of the immaculate conception 'is not *explicitly* revealed in Scripture'[2] and so we are asked to believe that it is '*implicitly*' contained in various passages. Thus the first great prophecy of the coming of the Saviour is cited: 'I will put enmity between you and the woman, and between your seed and her seed; he shall bruise your head, and you shall bruise his heel.'[3] But it is

[1] Lk. 1:34. [2] *Fundamentals of Catholic Dogma*, p. 200.
[3] Gn. 3:15.

121

surely rather fanciful to argue from this that 'Mary's victory over Satan would not have been perfect if she had ever been under his dominion. Consequently she must have entered this world without the stain of original sin.' [4] In any case the victory over Satan is not declared to be won by 'the woman' but by 'the seed of the woman', namely Christ.

We turn to the salutation of the angel, 'Hail, full of grace'.[5] The inference drawn from this is that Mary's sinlessness is implied in her being the special object of divine favour. But the self-same word,[6] used here of Mary, is used also in the Epistle to the Ephesians of the elect,[7] and is literally rendered by the Douay Version 'he hath graced us'. Yet we would never dream of arguing from the fact that God has thus 'graced us' that we are therefore immune from sin. It seems therefore completely inadmissible to read the dogma into the angelic message. This is confirmed by the alternative, and more correct, translation in the margin, 'Hail, O favoured one.' We might add further, lest anyone should imagine that the greeting 'hail' implies the meaning now given to its Latin equivalent 'Ave Maria', that it is well to recall that the word appears elsewhere in the New Testament as an ordinary mode of greeting.[8]

From the parallel between God's blessing upon Mary and upon the Child in Elizabeth's greeting, 'Blessed are you among women and blessed is the fruit of your womb',[9] the Roman Catholic Church infers that the mother shares the sinlessness of the Lord. This interpretation, if it were valid, would surely prove too much, for it leads to an attribution to the mother of all that is attributed to the Son, and Mary would share His divinity as well. But we do not need to adopt an interpretation which leads to such an impossible conclusion, for the interpretation itself is invalid. Elizabeth herself gives the reason for describing Mary as 'blessed', as she continues 'Blessed is she who believed'.[1] So it is not some alleged sinlessness which is a token of Mary's blessedness, but rather her readiness to believe

---

[4] *Op. cit.*, p. 200.   [5] Lk. 1:28.   [6] Greek *charitoō*.
[7] Eph. 1:6.   [8] See Mt. 26:49; 28:9; Acts 23:26.
[9] Lk. 1:42.   [1] Lk. 1:45.

122

the word of the Lord. It was her faith which marked her out as blessed. But this blessedness which is the mark of faith is not confined to Mary, for the Lord spoke of it in referring to those who would believe on Him. 'Blessed are those who have not seen and yet believe.' [2]

In opposition to any of these rather forced arguments are the plain words of Scripture. 'All have sinned and fall short of the glory of God.' [3] 'Death spread to all men because all men sinned.' [4] Of Christ alone is it ever expressly stated that He was 'without sin'.[5] Indeed the Virgin Mary is herself quite explicit on the subject. There is no doubt as to her own awareness of sin as she rejoices in knowing the God whom she describes as 'my Saviour'.[6] For the very title 'Saviour' speaks clearly of a salvation which is needed. When the birth of the Lord was announced He was descrîbed as the Saviour because He would 'save his people from their sins'.[7] When Mary therefore speaks of her Saviour she is confessing that she is simply one of those who need to be saved from their sins. If further confirmation of her own attitude is sought it may be found in her readiness to fulfil the Mosaic law of purification. Thus she goes to offer what is clearly described in the law [8] as being a sin offering which makes an atonement for her. It was not as one immaculate that Mary worshipped that day, but as a humble woman of God, acknowledging her need of a Saviour, and her indebtedness to the grace of God.

The appeal to tradition is as unavailing as the appeal to Scripture. Once again *'explicit'* mention is absent in the early centuries. It cannot be found earlier than in the fourth century and even then, only 'implicitly' in the analogy which Ephrem draws between Eve in her innocence and Mary in her sinlessness. But at once we recall that in Scripture the parallel is not Eve and Mary, but Adam and Christ!

---

[2] Jn. 20:29. The word here translated 'blessed' is the verb which corresponds to the adjective used by the Virgin in the Magnificat, 'All generations shall call me blessed'.

[3] Rom. 3:23.	[4] Rom. 5:12.	[5] Heb. 4:15.
[6] Lk. 1:47.	[7] Mt. 1:21.	[8] Lv. 12:6 ff.

123

A further attempt is made to read the dogma into the title 'Mother of God' given to Mary by the Council of Ephesus in AD 431. But one must remember the purpose of the title. The Council was resisting the error of Nestorius who was distinguishing so strongly between the two natures of Christ as to make virtually two persons. In order to emphasize the unity of the God-man, the Council stressed that He who was born of Mary was truly God. But in using this title 'Mother of God' it was the glory of the Son rather than of the mother that was in view.

The first real advocacy of the dogma comes in the twelfth century in the writing of a British monk Eadmer. But ranged against him in their denial of the dogma are names which are revered in the Church of Rome – Bernard of Clairvaux, Peter Lombard, Bonaventura, Thomas Aquinas. It was not until the fourteenth century that Duns Scotus elaborated the theory which was ultimately to win the day for the Franciscan advocates of the dogma in their debate with the Dominicans who had fiercely opposed it. According to this theory, Mary, as a child of Adam, was liable to original sin, but was, by divine intervention, kept from contracting its defilement. Hence the attempt is made to reconcile Mary's own expressed need of redemption with the dogma of the immaculate conception. Thus, it is claimed, Christ did redeem Mary, for it was on account of His merits that she was preserved free from original sin. Christians are redeemed from sin already present, but Mary was delivered from even contracting sin.

But this robs the cross of Christ of its essential meaning. Christ in His death 'bore our sins in his body on the tree'.[9] 'The Lord has laid on him the iniquity of us all.'[1] 'For our sake he made him to be sin who knew no sin.'[2] Here are typical statements of the nature of His atoning death. He truly bore our sins. But this teaching about Mary's being delivered from sin before contracting sin is a double contradiction. It is saying that she needed to be redeemed from something which she in no sense ever experienced; and when we realize that deliverance

[9] 1 Pet. 2:24.   [1] Is. 53:6.   [2] 2 Cor. 5:21.

or redemption is essentially deliverance from guilt and its penalty, we see how absurd is the idea of deliverance from a non-existent guilt. Furthermore, it means that she who never was in any real sense a sinner was saved, *i.e.* had her non-existent sins laid upon the Lord Jesus. It is quite clear what the apostle Paul means when he writes that Christ became 'a curse for us'; [3] He bore the curse of God which was due to us because of our sins. But if Mary was always free from sin she could not be subject to the curse of God, for to be accursed for a sin which never existed would be utterly unjust. The further failure in the theory is that it has a completely inadequate view of original sin. If this consists only in the lack of sanctifying grace, then it can be dealt with by a conferring of grace. But if sin is, as the Bible declares it to be, an offence against God, the wages of which are death, then sin inevitably means guilt, and redemption means pardon. If Mary was redeemed, as is freely accepted, then she had guilt to pardon. If she had guilt it was because of sin.

The dogma of the immaculate conception stands condemned at the bar of Scripture and of Christian history. If a final appeal is made to reason and the scholastic maxims are adduced: 'God could do it; God ought; therefore He did', we ask on what grounds is the assertion made 'God ought'? To say that it was fitting or appropriate or morally necessary that Mary should be conceived free of sin may have convinced Eadmer in the twelfth century, but it will hardly convince anyone today who takes Scripture seriously.

From her conception, we turn to her death, and here we meet the most recent dogma of the Roman Catholic Church, promulgated by Pope Pius XII in 1950. As defined by the Pope, speaking *ex cathedra*, and therefore with a full claim to infallibility, the dogma states that 'Mary the immaculate perpetually Virgin Mother of God, after the completion of her earthly life, was assumed body and soul into heaven'.

There is of course not a shred of evidence in the New Testament to sustain this dogma. It was unknown to the early

[3] Gal. 3:13.

125

Church which knew only of Mary's death. It is surely significant that since the sixth century in the East, and the seventh in
Rome, the feast of 'the Sleeping of Mary' was observed and by
this her death was acknowledged. It took the credulity of the
medieval scholastics to deduce, by the flimsiest arguments, the
incorruptibility and transfiguration of the body of Mary so that
the *dormitio* (sleeping) of Mary became the *assumptio*. They
base it on her supposed freedom from sin and her perpetual
virginity, a foundation of sand as we have seen. They claim
that her relationship to her Son demanded that in body and
soul she should be made like Him; but surely this would mean
not only resurrection but crucifixion! They attribute to her
such a share in the work of redemption, that it was only appropriate that she should share in the resurrection of the body
which is one of the fruits of that redemption. This last claim
is a far-reaching one and ushers us into a further field of discussion, as we consider Mary's alleged co-operation in the work
of redemption.

This co-operation is seen first in the part she played in the
incarnation of the Lord. Here a great deal is made of her
consent to the word of God through the angel, concerning the
miraculous birth: 'Behold, I am the handmaid of the Lord;
let it be to me according to your word.' [4] In this word of assent
it is claimed that Mary, having considered the divine proposal,
and having freely given her consent, became a vital link in the
plan of salvation, so that in fact the whole plan hung upon her
consent. But when we examine the context we get no hint of a
proposal by God. It is not a request but a sovereign declaration
of a divine purpose already formed. It is not 'Will you?', but,
'you will'. Furthermore, while fully acknowledging the faith
and obedience of Mary in her assent to God's will, we would
point out that to make this the grounds for claiming her as
co-redemptrix, is to raise the question of the role of Joseph.
After all, the life of the infant Jesus hung upon his obedience
to the call to flee into Egypt. Indeed we must go further and
see a like importance in the obedience of the Wise Men. Are

[4] Lk. 1:38.

Joseph and the Wise Men also to be accorded the status given to Mary? What indeed are we to say about Judas Iscariot whose disobedience was as vital a factor in the outworking of the plan as was the obedience of others?

What then is our reply to the assertion that Mary gave to the world the Redeemer, or that Mary on Golgotha offered Him to the Father? The answer is quite plain. The giving is firmly declared to be by the Father. It was not Mary but God who 'so loved the world, that he gave his only Son'; [5] it was God who 'sent forth his Son'.[6] And Scripture is equally plain about the offering at Golgotha. Jesus Himself was quite explicit; 'I lay down my life . . . I lay it down of my own accord'.[7] There is an echo of this in Hebrews which speaks of Christ 'who . . . offered himself'.[8]

But Mary's lofty role in Roman Catholic devotion does not depend only on her part in the incarnation, but perhaps even more on her present position in heaven. Here, enthroned as Queen, she intercedes for her children, and the very relationship which she sustains to Christ makes this intercession especially powerful. Leo XIII could go so far as to say in the *Rosary Encyclical* of 1891, 'From that great treasure of all graces which the Lord has brought, nothing according to the will of God comes to us except through Mary, so that, as nobody can approach the Supreme Father except through the Son, similarly nobody can approach Christ except through the Mother.' Pope Pius X (1903–1914) echoes this teaching in the claim that Mary is 'the dispenser of all gifts which Jesus has acquired for us by His death and His blood'. Pope Benedict XV (1914–1922) calls her 'the mediatrix with God of all graces'.

Again Ludwig Ott has the frankness to say: 'Express scriptural proofs are lacking.' [9] But the Protestant goes further, and says that express scriptural refutation is by no means lacking! Paul writes to Timothy, 'there is one God, and there is one mediator between God and men, the man Christ Jesus'.[1] The Lord Himself makes His great claim, 'I am the way, and the

[5] Jn. 3:16.   [6] Gal. 4:4.   [7] Jn. 10:15, 17, 18.
[8] Heb. 9:14.   [9] *Op. cit.*, p. 214.   [1] 1 Tim. 2:5.

truth, and the life. No one comes to the Father, but by me.'[2] Nor does He qualify this by assigning a subsidiary mediatorship to Mary, for He calls men directly to Himself. 'Come to me, all who labour and are heavy laden';[3] and He rebukes the Jews on this very count, 'you refuse to come to me that you may have life'.[4] The apostle John writes in a similar fashion; 'if any man sin, we have an advocate with the Father, Jesus Christ the righteous'.[5] This is the One, says the Epistle to the Hebrews, who 'is able for all time to save those who draw near to God through him'.[6]

It is easy to see the attraction of this call to go through Mary to Christ, for she is pictured as the sympathetic woman who understands our needs. But again Scripture is quite plain. The great thing, says Paul, about this mediator between God and men is that He 'is a man, like them'.[7] This thought is greatly expanded in the Epistle to the Hebrews, where stress is laid on the sympathy of our Saviour. 'Therefore he had to be made like his brethren in every respect, so that he might become a merciful and faithful high priest in the service of God.'[8] In face of the appeal to the motherly sympathy of Mary we maintain that such an appeal does despite to the perfect sympathy of Christ. Hebrews has an answer that might have been given specifically for this situation. 'For we have not a high priest who is unable to sympathize with our weaknesses, but one who in every respect has been tempted as we are, yet without sinning. Let us then with confidence draw near to the throne of grace.'[9]

The development of Mariology has been accompanied by an ever-increasing tendency to accord to Mary a worship that, in much popular devotion, is indistinguishable from that offered to God Himself. It is true that the Roman Catholic theologian distinguishes between the 'adoration' (*latria*) which is due to God alone; the 'veneration' (*dulia*) which is offered to the saints; and the 'special veneration' (*hyperdulia*) which is given to Mary. But this is a distinction which is not only utterly absent from

[2] Jn. 14:6.   [3] Mt. 11:28.   [4] Jn. 5:40.
[5] 1 Jn. 2:1.   [6] Heb. 7:25.   [7] 1 Tim. 2:5 (Knox).
[8] Heb. 2:17.   [9] Heb. 4:15f.

Scripture, but is virtually impossible to maintain in practice. When the average Roman Catholic invokes the aid of 'Jesus, Mary and Joseph' it is hard to conceive that he distinguishes, in a split second, between *latria*, *hyperdulia* and *dulia*!

The theologian may complain that he cannot be blamed for the extremes of popular devotion. But he is in fact guilty if, seeing the error, he does not repudiate it; and he is even more fundamentally blameworthy if it is his own teaching which leads to the error. Now Rome may be indicted on both these counts. Far from putting a brake on the cult of Mary, the powers that be have accelerated its growth. The declaration at Vatican II that Mary is the mother of the Church is one more illustration of this. Then, too, their teaching has led inevitably to the popular cult. Rome may deny that Mary is worshipped as God. But to attribute to her powers which involve omniscience and omnipresence, if she is to hear the prayers of millions, is to accord to her what belongs to God alone. Furthermore, the prayers themselves are phrased in such a way that it is hard to distinguish them from those offered to God. It is well-nigh impossible to see what distinction may be made between a prayer to God for deliverance, and that which comes in the Litany of the Blessed Virgin, 'We fly to thy patronage O holy Mother of God; despise not our prayers in our necessities, but deliver us from all dangers, O ever glorious and blessed Virgin.' To accord to the Virgin, among a multitude of other exalted titles, such ascriptions as Mirror of Justice; Seal of Wisdom; Tower of David; Ark of the Covenant; Gate of Heaven; Queen of Angels, Patriarchs, Prophets, Apostles, Martyrs – this surely is going far beyond the bounds of truth. It is a significant comment on all this that in the popular use of the rosary the 'hail Mary' is said a great deal more often than the Lord's Prayer!

The whole system of Mariology is strangely remote from the actual pattern which emerges in the New Testament, both in its positive references and in its equally impressive silences. Taking the latter first, it would be hard to find a greater contrast than that between the constant reference to Mary in modern Roman

Catholic pronouncements, and the utter and complete absence of even the mention of her name in the New Testament Epistles. These letters were written for the guidance of the Churches, and have much to say, not only about doctrine, but about Church order and worship. But Mary's name is entirely absent. Can we imagine a series of letters sent by a Roman Catholic bishop today to cover every aspect of Church life without even a single mention of Mary?

It would of course be precarious to base a position entirely on the argument from silence; but the positive statements of the New Testament lead overwhelmingly to the same conclusions. Mary herself is concerned to magnify not herself but the Lord. Her honour in being the mother of the Lord is entirely due to the One who has done for her great things.

But Mary was very human, and was thus in danger of overstepping the bounds of what was legitimate. Hence she needed the gentle but firm rebuke of the Lord. Even in the early days when He was still a boy there is this note. In reply to Mary's expostulation of pained surprise that He should have stayed behind in Jerusalem, and thus caused her and Joseph much anxiety, He answers, 'How is it that you sought me? Did you not know that I must be in my Father's house?' [1]

This note of gentle rebuke comes more strongly in the account of His first miracle which He performed at Cana in Galilee.[2] Mary, clearly conscious of His true nature, comes to Him with the difficulty 'They have no wine'. His reply is quite respectful – the term 'Woman' did not imply any disrespect; but it is also quite firm. 'O woman, what have you to do with me? My hour has not yet come.' Knox gives, as an apt paraphrase of this, 'Leave me alone, do not interfere with me'; and clearly we hear the Lord reminding His mother that she must not try to claim an authority which God never intended she should have.

The same kind of rebuke, this time administered in an indirect way, comes in the account of the visit of His mother and His brothers. They stand outside the house, and ask to see Him.

[1] Lk. 2:49.   [2] Jn. 2:1–11.

But instead of speaking of her exalted status, He takes the opportunity of teaching the crowd an important lesson. 'Who,' he asks, 'are my mother and my brothers?' And, looking round on these who sat about him, he said: 'Here are my mother and my brothers! Whoever does the will of God is my brother, and sister, and mother.'[3] Here surely is the Lord's answer to all the Roman claims for Mary. Her glory was that she did the will of God, and that glory is one that any humble but obedient Christian may, by the grace of God, share.

There is an echo of the 'Hail Mary' in the cry of the woman recorded by Luke,[4] 'Blessed is the womb that bore you, and the breasts that you sucked!' Here surely was the occasion for the Lord to endorse such a eulogy of praise to the Virgin. But on the contrary He rejects it. Again His theme is that the one who obeys the word of God is equally blessed with Mary. Indeed, by the way He puts His reply – 'Blessed rather are those who hear the word of God and keep it' – He is emphasizing that the essential thing about Mary was her obedience, and this is something which is not peculiar to her, but should indeed be a characteristic of every believer.

The Lord had undoubtedly a deep affection for His mother. Even in His dying moments on the cross, He showed His concern for her welfare as He committed her to the protection of the beloved apostle John.[5] Some have tried to interpret this in a mystical way as a declaration of Mary's motherhood over the Church represented by John. But the context makes it plain that it was intended quite literally, and John certainly took it in that way for he at once provided Mary with a home. Here, then, is the Lord's love for Mary seen in action. It is the concern which any true son would show for his mother in such circumstances. But, as we have seen, Christ never allows His respect and affection for her to mislead either her or others into thinking that to her belongs some special status not shared by His other disciples.

Mariology is particularly significant in that we meet here the supreme illustration of the Roman Catholic view of man. Be-

[3] Mk. 3:33–35.　　　[4] Lk. 11:27f.　　　[5] Jn. 19:26ff.

131

hind the idea of Mary's co-operation in the work of redemption is the Catholic view of human ability and Rome's teaching on the possibility and indeed the necessity of human merit. Thus Sebastian Bullough in the Pelican book, *Roman Catholicism*, writes 'Since Christ is both God and man it was fitting that mankind in the person of Mary should have co-operated with God in the work of salvation by the incarnation of the Word of God when Mary freely accepted the task of being the Saviour's mother.'[6] Yves Congar, a leading progressive, adopts the same position, that Mariology and ecclesiology are inseparable, for in Mary we see supremely the element of co-operation in the work of redemption which we see now in the Church. Thus he writes, 'It cannot be denied that in Jesus Christ heaven and earth are united. . . . But in setting up this union of heaven and earth accomplished in person by Jesus Christ, a share is also to be attributed to our Lady through her co-operation in the mystery of the Incarnation, and to the Church because it communicates to us the effects which flow from the Incarnation. . . . Here then it may be reiterated, is a meeting point upon which our Lady and the Church conclusively and positively converge; each, that is, represents the part that human instrumentality is given in the work of salvation through the Incarnation; the one brings it about, the other communicates it to men and permeates the world with its effects.'[7]

Subilia trenchantly observes that Mariolatry clearly shows how false is Küng's contention that Rome really teaches justification by faith. Were this so she would have rejected Mariolatry with its emphasis on human merit and co-operation. Her continued acceptance of Mariolatry and indeed her whole-hearted propagation of this error demonstrates that it is the old traditional interpretation of Trent with its stress on human merit which is the correct one, and Küng's attempt to make Trent teach *sola fide* (by faith alone) involves him here in inconsistency.

A consideration of Mariolatry is also important because of

[6] P. 151.   [7] *Christ, our Lady and the Church*, p. 15.

its symptomatic value, for it reveals the true position within Rome. Thus John, the ecumenical Pope, put the Council under the protection of Mary, 'the Immaculate Queen of the Church and mother of unity'.[8] In his address of 15 February 1959, he stated, 'It is through Mary that we come to Jesus, to love Christ means to love Mary His mother and in the light of redemption our universal mother.' Cardinal Heenan in his speech at Vatican II on ecumenism in England and Wales said, 'Let all therefore, both Catholics and the separated brethren, so dear to us, strive that under the protection of Mary, the mother of God, the coming of the Kingdom of God in the unity of the Church may soon be brought nearer.'[9] Pope Paul VI, as we know, crowned all this by declaring Mary to be 'the mother of the Church'.

But the new theologians do not lag behind. While Küng did express the hope that no further Marian dogmas would be added – a hope that in the event was largely nullified by Paul's action – he has also written, 'Can we be Christians without being Marian? Can we make a Christian theology without making a Marian one? Could any return to unity be possible if one turns one's back on the mystery of Mary'.[1]

Another of the new theologians, Schillebeeckx, the adviser to the Dutch bishops at Vatican II, has written a book on the subject – *Mary the Mother of the Redemption.* Here are the old arguments refurbished with an appearance of biblical justification – Redemption by exemption; Mary's fiat, *i.e.* her word of acceptance which was the necessary prerequisite for the work of Christ; Mary as embodying the hope of Israel; Mary as the mother of the church – clearly we have not moved at all from the dogmas of 1854 and 1950 and Mariolatry is as firmly entrenched as ever. When a progressive can write, 'The natural quality of love cannot be in the man Jesus – but it is in Mary,'[2] or again, 'Together with Mary and under her influence we encounter Christ the man directly,'[3] we can see how closely

[8] January 25 1959.
[9] *Council Speeches of Vatican II*, p. 108.
[1] H. Küng, *The Council and Reunion* (Sheed & Ward, 1961), p. 187.   [2] P. 142.   [3] P. 180.

identified in this vital theological issue the new theologians are with the traditional Roman conservatives. In view of the ecumenical trend of the day it is good to remember the wording of the papal bull of 1854 declaring the Immaculate Conception of Mary – 'if any should presume to think in their hearts otherwise than as it has been defined by us, which God avert, let them know and understand that they are condemned by their own judgment; that they have suffered shipwreck in regard to faith'.

The decree of Vatican II on the Church both emphasizes the old position and develops it further in an unbiblical direction. She is 'the glorious Mary ever virgin'. She is 'all-holy and free from every stain of sin'. She 'co-operated with unconstrained faith and obedience in the salvation of man'. She 'was raised, body and soul, to the glory of heaven. She has been exalted by the Lord as Queen of all.' As a consequence of this she is 'called upon in the Church under the titles of Advocate, Auxiliatrix, Adjutrix, Mediatrix'.[4] She is the mother of the faithful for 'she co-operates in their generation and education with all the love of a mother'. Catholics should 'give generous encouragement to the cult of the Blessed Virgin'. Throughout the decree with its adulation of Mary and her proclamation as mother of the faithful we see the recurring failure to distinguish between the physical body of Jesus and His spiritual body which is the Church. It is an utterly false transition from the physical relationship of Mary to Jesus, to a spiritual relationship with those who are Christ's by the miracle of the new birth brought about by the Holy Spirit.

As we saw in an earlier chapter the Roman Catholic charismatic movement is also strongly committed in the same direction. It is far from unusual to hear those who claim the baptism in the Spirit profess that one result of their new experience is a deeper devotion to Mary. The devotional use of the rosary has been stimulated rather than curtailed. The teaching of Vatican II on Mary as the mother of the Church has been firmly endorsed by the claim that because she was present on the

[4] See glossary.

day of Pentecost she co-operated with the Spirit in the birth of the Church, just as she had done in the incarnation of Christ – a false analogy, as we have already seen.

It is one of the tragedies of Christian history that Mary, whose humility and obedience shine so clearly, should have been loaded with honours from which she would have recoiled in horror. The 'Mary' of Roman Catholic theology is far removed from the Mary of the New Testament. The former has her origin in the Roman Catholic view of man with his capacity to receive grace, so that this 'Mary' is the supreme illustration of Roman teaching on the place of human merit.[5] The true Mary is an illustration rather of the grace of God which stoops to sinful men. She appears as a woman of simple faith and obedience, whose memory we recall with thanksgiving to God, and whose submission to the sovereign will of God we seek to make our own.

[5] See G. C. Berkouwer, *The Conflict with Rome* (Presbyterian & Reformed Publishing Co., Philadelphia, 1958), p. 166.

13

Penance

There is no doubt that the Church of Rome takes sin seriously and in this, as in other points, shows a healthy divergence from the shallow optimism of liberal theology. Sin is seen to be the greatest evil in the world. It is essentially law breaking, and so inevitably brings consequences. But as the law which is broken is not some human code, but the law of God, the consequences are correspondingly serious. Here again Rome sounds a clear note of warning as she emphasizes that hell is no myth but a solemn reality; and doubtless anyone who has listened to the mission preaching of the Redemptorists will know how strongly such a warning can be enforced.

Rome's grasp of the gravity of sin can be seen also in her whole sacramental system which is essentially her answer (or, as she would claim, God's answer) to this basic problem. This reply, however, finds its most explicit expression in the 'sacrament' of penance in which sin is dealt with. While we shall have occasion to criticize her teaching at this point, we would readily acknowledge that, although we believe her solution to be wrong, she yet shows a true awareness that the problem is of such magnitude that an answer must be found.

While Rome insists that all sins are an offence against God, yet she distinguishes between greater and lesser sins, which are thus classified as 'mortal' and 'venial'. A mortal sin is one which brings with it spiritual death, and so is a sin which cuts a man off from God now, and if it is not pardoned, will cut him off eternally. A venial sin (from the Latin word *venia* which means 'pardon') is one which is less serious, and is more easily pardoned. Mortal sins embrace such transgressions as the breaking of the Ten Commandments; the seven deadly sins – pride, covetousness, lust, anger, gluttony, envy, sloth; sexual offences; missing mass; and, of course, many others. A hasty word or carelessness in prayer would fall in the category of venial sins.

The problem of course is to distinguish between what is mortal and what is venial. For a sin to be mortal it must be a serious matter, and must be done consciously and deliberately. But what constitutes a 'serious matter'? Ever since Eden man has been an adept at excusing himself, and the whole idea of less serious offences is one which gives him abundant scope for attempting to evade the judgment of a Holy God upon every sin.

Rome would claim that this distinction is a common-sense one. There is a difference surely between a hasty word and murder! But while it is true that there is a difference as far as the consequences are concerned, there is no difference in the sight of God between one sin and another as far as guilt is concerned. When Paul declares 'the wages of sin is death' [1] he draws no distinction between one sin and another. James is even more emphatic in his rejection of the idea that any sin is venial: 'For whoever keeps the whole law but fails in one point has become guilty of all of it.' [2]

It will not do to appeal to the apostle John who speaks of 'sin which is mortal' [3] for this would prove too much. A mortal sin for Rome is one which can be forgiven, and for which therefore pardon should be sought. But the sin of which John speaks is one of such a serious character that he cannot even ask his hearers to pray for one who is guilty of it. It would seem therefore that he is referring to such a sin as apostasy, or final and persistent impenitence – the sin against the Holy Spirit for which the Lord says there is no forgiveness – and this is, in fact, recognized in the note in the Douay Version.

The distinction made by the Roman Catholic Church is surely both morally and spiritually dangerous. For the careless it leads all too easily to a perilous state of self-deception. For the earnest seeker there is an inevitable uncertainty. How can

[1] Rom. 6:23.   [2] Jas. 2:10.   [3] 1 Jn. 5:16.

he be sure that his assessment is correct? Perhaps those sins which he thought were venial, and consequently omitted from his confession to the priest, were after all mortal, and being unconfessed bring hell as a judgment. His way out of this impasse is further bondage, for he must rely on the priest who professes to be the expert on questions of moral theology. But even then he is not out of the wood, for the debates among the moral theologians show the areas of uncertainty in their own thinking. The only safe course would be to treat what may seem to be venial sins as mortal, and to confess all, so that the net result is the increasing domination of the confessional.

But even in the matter of confessing sin Rome introduces a distinction between what she calls 'attrition' and 'contrition'. The former is confession of an inferior kind. It is produced not by love for God or by hatred of sin as that which is displeasing to God, but by some lesser motive such as fear of hell. Attrition is adequate to deal with venial sins; but to deal with mortal sins it must be supplemented by the confessional. Contrition is much more the biblical attitude of repentance and, in theory, is sufficient to meet the consequences of mortal sins. Contrition is defined by the Council of Trent as 'Grief of the soul for and detestation of the sins committed, with the intention not to sin in future'. But even here the confessional lies in the background, for while a sincere act of contrition is sufficient when recourse cannot be had to the priest, yet it is held that such an act inevitably implies a resolve to confess to the priest as soon as there is an opportunity.

But Scripture gives no grounds for this distinction between a perfect and imperfect contrition. The classic statement of repentance in Psalm 51 (50), sees sin as being loathsome because it is an offence against God, and sees sin's consequences as being a loss of God's favour. Thus repentance is not simply a self-centred attitude begotten of the fear of the punishment due to sin. It is rather an aversion from sin which springs from a desire for God's favour. In the New Testament the apostle Paul knits together repentance to God with faith in our Lord

138

Jesus Christ.[4] The call in the New Testament is to 'repent and believe in the gospel'.[5] To separate repentance from faith is to produce an attitude which bears no relationship to the authentic sorrow of the sinner. Attrition, in other words, is not repentance at all; it is simply an expression of self-love. It is perfectly true that the fear of hell may awaken the sinner from his slumbers; but if it is not allied to a fear of God, it remains as barren as it was for King Saul or Judas Iscariot. Godly sorrow, says the apostle Paul, 'leads to an abiding and salutary change of heart, whereas the world's remorse leads to death'.[6] True repentance is not man-centred but God-centred, and to give any place to such a conception as attrition, is once again to open the door to what may appear to be the pathway to pardon, but is in fact a spiritual blind alley.

These distinctions between venial and mortal sins and between attrition and contrition introduce us to the heart of Roman teaching on penance which, as we have seen, is declared to be a sacrament. It is made quite clear that sacramental confession before a priest in order to obtain his pardon is not something which may or may not be practised as the penitent may decide. It is not merely a means of relief for those whose burdened consciences cannot find peace. It is rather, in Roman Catholic doctrine, ordained by God and necessary for salvation.

In the sacraments of baptism and the Lord's Supper it is easy to distinguish the 'matter', that is the material element used, and the 'form', namely the Trinitarian formula in baptism or the words of institution in the Communion. But judged by this standard, how are we to find 'matter' and 'form' in this 'sacrament' of penance? Rome's answer is that the 'matter' of the sacrament is the confession made by the penitent which, as we have seen, may be only attrition, while the 'form' is the words of absolution pronounced by the priest.

It is essential to an understanding of Rome's whole approach that we should grasp the role of the priest in the confessional. He is not there simply to declare God's forgiveness, and so to

4 Acts 20:21.   5 Mk. 1:15.
6 2 Cor. 7:10 (Knox).

give the assurance of pardon which the burdened sinner needs. His is a much more authoritative position for he acts as a judge, and in fact the confessional is called the 'tribunal of penance'. The priest claims to have judicial power and, on examination of the penitent, to be able to pronounce a sentence which actually remits or retains sins. The formula 'I absolve thee' (*ego te absolvo*) is no empty one, but implies the full power of the judge.

As judge, the priest not only gives forgiveness but also imposes penance. The word in this context is used in the more restricted sense of acts of piety which the penitent is required to carry out. Again it must be stressed that the penance imposed is not simply a means of testing the genuineness of the confession but is by way of satisfaction offered to God. The sinner has affronted God's holiness and therefore, it is claimed, he faces a double consequence. There is the eternal punishment in hell which is the penalty due to the guilty sinner, and it is this which is averted when the guilt is removed by the priestly absolution. But there is also the temporal punishment which remains after the guilt and its eternal punishment have been dealt with. Hence sin must still be atoned for by penance which is a satisfaction offered to the offended justice of God and is, as it were, an act of reparation for the wrong done. This penance is performed either by means of good works in this life or via the suffering endured in purgatory.

But, as we saw earlier when considering the nature of the priesthood, there is not the slightest hint in the New Testament of such a compulsory confession to a priest. Dr Ott is again quite candid. 'The Divine institution and the necessity for salvation of the particular confession of sins is not explicitly stated in Holy Writ.' Indeed he goes even further and admits that 'the passages 1 John 1:9; James 5:16; Acts 19:18, which refer to a confession of sins, do not necessarily refer to a sacramental acknowledgment of sins; in fact they probably do not'.[7]

Clearly in the New Testament there is provision for confession to a fellow Christian when we have sinned against him.

[7] *Op. cit.*, p. 431.

There is provision, too, for confession to the Church when our sin has been a cause of offence to the community of believers. But of confession to a priest there is not a word. There is too much emphasis on the sole mediatorship of Christ to allow for any human mediators. The call to come boldly to the throne of grace is issued to all believers, and the blessing offered is precisely that which the priest claims to offer in the confessional, namely, 'mercy' and 'grace'.[8]

Appeal is made to the Lord's promise to Peter, 'I will give you the keys of the kingdom of heaven, and whatever you bind on earth shall be bound in heaven, and whatever you loose on earth shall be loosed in heaven.' [9] But surely the outworking of this is seen not in Peter's exercising a priestly ministry of absolution in the confessional, but by his preaching of the gospel. Thus at the Council of Jerusalem he recalls how God had opened the door of faith to the Gentiles through the words of his lips.[1] But these words, as recorded earlier in Acts,[2] were not a judicial sentence pronounced over Cornelius, but a preaching of the gospel leading to the declaration, 'Every one who believes in him receives forgiveness of sins through his name.' Thus Peter, by his preaching, used the keys of the kingdom to open the door to men of faith. But coupled with his preaching was his apostolic authority. Hence, when he spoke of pardon to those who repented, he did so with the authority of the Lord. When he declared to Simon Magus [3] that he was still in sin he spoke with the same authority. But in both cases it was the authority of one who declares God's absolution rather than of one who effects it by his own power. The authority of God rests both on his preaching and on his words of reassurance to the penitent and of rejection of the impenitent. This is the same authority which enables the Church to reinforce such words of welcome or rejection by the exercise of a godly discipline.

Appeal is also made to the Lord's commission to His disciples after the resurrection: 'Receive the Holy Spirit. If you forgive the sins of any, they are forgiven; if you retain the sins

[8] Heb. 4:16. [9] Mt. 16:19. [1] Acts 15:7.
[2] Acts 10:34–43. [3] Acts 8:23.

of any, they are retained.'[4] But at once we notice that the apostles were not alone in receiving this commission, for other disciples were with them. In Luke's account of the incident there are not only the eleven apostles, but also their companions, as well as the two who had been on the road to Emmaus and who had just joined them when the Lord appeared. Judging by the enumeration of those present in the upper room shortly afterwards[5] the company probably included Mary the mother of Jesus and the rest of the women. This is confirmed by John's account, where Mary Magdalene joins them immediately prior to the Lord's appearance and declaration. But all this easily falls into the New Testament pattern, for we find later that not only did the apostles preach, and so with authority declare the remission of sins, but all the believers 'went about preaching the word'.[6] The authority conferred by Christ was not confined to some priestly caste, but was given to the whole Church.

How then is this commission to be discharged? The clue is to be found in verse 21 'as my Father has sent me even so I send you'. Here is the great commission paralleled by Matthew 28:19-20 or Acts 1:8. This 'sending' was with a view to spreading the gospel. They are to go into all the world and preach the gospel to every creature. Those who receive the Word are to be baptized and taught the whole counsel of God.

But there is a further word of reassurance. They are being sent with a divinely-given authority. Their message is from God and so they speak with assurance. When they preach the forgiveness of sins there is no 'maybe' or 'perhaps'; there is a note of certainty. And it is in this context that we must see the meaning of the word: 'If you forgive the sins of any they are forgiven; if you retain the sins of any they are retained.' They are not simply to tell about forgiveness and judgment they are to declare them with authority.

Now since this commission was not simply one for the apostles but is given to the Church, it is an abiding one today.

[4] Jn. 20:22f   [5] Acts 1:14;   [6] Acts 8:4;

This ministry of 'forgiving' and 'retaining' continues among us. It is exercised in the preaching of the gospel when the humble seeker is assured, on the basis of the promises of God, that he has forgiveness. It is exercised when the new born believer is baptized. In the ordinance he is being assured of the reality of the new birth with the accompanying remission of sins. It is exercised in the administration of a godly discipline. The penitent who turns from his sins is welcomed into fellowship with a declaration of forgiveness pronounced by the Church but ratified by the Lord. When the impenitent is excluded from fellowship the declaration that his 'sins are retained' is made by the Church which simply echoes the Word of the Lord.

There is one important factor which must not be forgotten. The prelude to the Lord's call to exercise this authoritative ministry was His gift of the Holy Spirit. It is only a Spirit-filled Church which can hope to discharge this commission. A worldly-minded Church may declare the forgiveness of sins lightly so that those who have made a nominal profession are assured when they ought to be checked and warned. A Church relying on human wisdom rather than on the Spirit of God may include men whom the Lord will exclude, and may exclude those whom the Lord will include. The power of the Spirit is a continuing necessity in the carrying out of the commission of the Lord.

What, then, of the teaching that satisfaction must be offered to atone for those temporal consequences of sin which remain even after pardon has been given? The answer to this is the New Testament stress on the completeness of the pardon given by God in view of the perfect satisfaction offered by Christ. It is perfectly true, of course, that the temporal consequences often remain even after sin has been confessed and pardoned. A man who has lived a loose life will bear in his body the ravages of past misdeeds even though he himself is pardoned by God. Another who has been an evil influence before his conversion will have the grief of seeing the ill results of the past still persisting in the lives of others. The sins of earlier years

143

may hinder a man later from embarking on some field of service for God. But in all these cases we must surely distinguish between God's attitude prior to repentance and subsequently. The guilty sinner is under God's judgment and the wrath of God is a solemn reality. But with God's pardon there is restoration to favour. The Psalmist can pray in his plea for forgiveness: 'Restore to me the joy of thy salvation'.[7] The prophet likewise brings a word which is, as it were, God's reply to such a cry: 'I will heal their faithlessnesses; I will love them freely: for my anger has turned from them.'[8] God may in chastening love leave us to live with the consequences of our sins, so that He may humble us and teach us how completely we are in debt to His grace. But as far as His displeasure is concerned, there can be no continuance of this when He has freely pardoned us.

The apostle John speaks of the completeness of God's pardon as he writes: 'If we confess our sins, he is faithful and just, and will forgive our sins and cleanse us from all unrighteousness.'[9] Indeed he has already stressed this point that the blood of His Son Jesus Christ 'cleanses us from all sin'.[1] Here is an echo of the Old Testament promises, 'Though your sins are like scarlet they shall be as white as snow; though they are red like crimson, they shall become like wool.'[2] 'I have swept away your transgressions like a cloud, and your sins like mist; return to me for I have redeemed you.'[3]

The whole idea of a continuing punishment for sin for which satisfaction must be offered does despite to the perfection of Christ's atoning death. To say that I, by the performance of penance, or by the suffering of purgatory, must satisfy the offended justice of God, is to say that Christ's offering has not adequately met God's just demands. Otherwise it would be unjust to exact a satisfaction for sin if that satisfaction had already been made.

But Christ's satisfaction is surely perfect. His offering, after all, was provided by the Father. Thus Paul writes of the

[7] Ps. 51 (50):12   [8] Ho. 14:5.   [9] 1 Jn. 1:9.
[1] 1 Jn. 1:7.   [2] Is. 1:18.   [3] Is. 44:22.

144

Saviour 'whom God put forward as an expiation by his blood'.[4] 'He', says John, 'is the expiation for our sins.'[5] His present position at the right hand of God is a clear declaration that the propitiation He has offered has been accepted. God's justice has been satisfied, and the guilty sinner needs a humble reliance upon Christ alone.

The apostle Paul, indeed, goes further and rules out any possibility of human merit. 'For by grace you have been saved through faith; and this is not your own doing, it is the gift of God – not because of works, lest any man should boast.'[6] This means that the good works which follow our acceptance by God must never be seen as a meritorious satisfaction. Rather they are, on the one hand, the indication of the reality of our profession of faith and, on the other, the grateful offering of those who realize that the aim of God in our salvation is that we should live holy lives. 'For we are his workmanship, created in Christ Jesus for good works, which God prepared beforehand that we should walk in them.'[7]

The Christian does not live under the partial cloud of a punishment yet to be experienced. He knows rather the confidence of the apostle that 'there is therefore now no condemnation for those who are in Christ Jesus'.[8] Having been accepted for Christ's sake, he knows not only 'peace with God' but the unclouded joy which accompanies such an assurance of a complete pardon grounded in the all-sufficient merits and the perfectly accomplished atonement of our blessed Lord Jesus Christ.[9]

[4] Rom. 3:25. [5] 1 Jn. 2:2. [6] Eph. 2:8f.
[7] Eph. 2:10. [8] Rom. 8:1. [9] Rom. 5:1–3.

14

Indulgences

In the early Church discipline was much more strongly administered than in these days of laxity. If a Christian sinned in such a grievous fashion as to cause offence to the Church, he was liable to be suspended from communion and this excommunication could be for longer or shorter periods of time according to the decision of the Church. It was of course possible for the punishment to be mitigated. Perhaps the penitent showed clear and unmistakable evidence of true repentance, or it might be that some believer who had undergone great suffering in days of persecution interceded for him. Whatever the grounds for their decision, it was quite possible for the Church to remit part of the sentence which they had themselves imposed, and in this sense the penitent was granted an indulgence.

Now quite obviously we can have no quarrel with an indulgence which means the remission, in whole or in part, of a penalty imposed by the Church as a matter of discipline. After all, we see this very thing happening at Corinth. Paul writes and counsels against undue severity towards the offender. To make the sentence too stiff, and to prolong it unduly, is to run the risk of driving the sinner to despair. So the apostle argues that he should be restored to fellowship. 'For such a one this punishment by the majority is enough; so you should rather turn to forgive and comfort him, or he may be overwhelmed by excessive sorrow.' [1]

But the Roman doctrine of indulgences goes far beyond any mere remission of an ecclesiastical penalty, for it is concerned

[1] 2 Cor. 2:6–8.

with the punishment imposed, not by a Church, but by God Himself. As we saw earlier, the claim is made that in the confessional the guilt of mortal sin is removed by the absolution of the priest, but the temporal consequences of the sin remain. The expiation or reparation required is met partly by good works on the part of the penitent and partly by his suffering after death the pains of purgatory. Now it is precisely these penal consequences for which an indulgence is granted. It must therefore be stressed at the outset that an indulgence is not, in Rome's view, the remission of sin in the sense of pardon, but is rather a remission of the temporal punishments for sin imposed by God. An indulgence may be partial or plenary, the difference being that between a partial and a complete remission of the punishment of the penitent.

There is a distinction drawn between the granting of indulgences to the living and to the departed. In the case of the former, he must be in a state of grace, that is, he must have confessed his sin, received absolution, and must have performed the required penance. In such a case the indulgence is granted to him directly by the Church with an authoritative declaration of remission. But in the case of the departed the application of the indulgence is indirect, in that it is granted in response to the plea of one who is still alive and acts for his departed friend. In this case there is not the same note of assurance concerning indulgences, and indeed 'their operation is uncertain'.[2] We will return to this matter when we deal with the doctrine of purgatory.[3]

Lying behind this claim to be able to dispense indulgences is the conception of the treasury of merit, which is itself an outgrowth of the teaching concerning works of supererogation. Such works are those performed by the saints over and above the normal requirements. Since, in Rome's view, good works are meritorious, and indeed are required as penance for sin, it is considered possible for those of exceptional sanctity not only to offer a penance sufficient for their own needs but to acquire

[2] Ludwig Ott, *Fundamentals of Catholic Dogma*, p. 444.
[3] See chapter 16.

additional merits by the good works which are over and above (Latin *super*) what God asks (Latin *rogo*); hence the description, 'works of supererogation'.

These superabundant merits of the saints are added to the infinite merits of Christ to form the treasury of merit on which the Church may draw for the benefit of the faithful. The justification for this alleged transference of merit from the heavenly bank to the penitent's account is the 'communion of saints'. Christians, it is claimed, being one body, may enter into an enjoyment of benefits earned by other members of the body.

The treasury of merit comes under the authority of the Pope. With his claim to have the power of the keys, he exercises jurisdiction. Thus it is ultimately the Pope who dispenses indulgences. The priest who may deal with the penitent and grant him an indulgence does so only as the agent of the Pope who claims to have supreme authority in this matter. The bishops may also dispense indulgences but only within strictly defined limits. To the Pope alone belongs absolute control over the heavenly treasury, from which he dispenses as he wills.

But what has Scripture to say about this idea of works of supererogation? The answer surely comes with a humbling clarity in the Lord's own words to His disciples. He quotes the example of a servant who acts in obedience to his master's commands, and asks 'Does he thank the servant because he did what was commanded?' Then the Lord adds His comment with its application to the disciples – 'So you also, when you have done all that is commanded you, say, "We are unworthy servants; we have only done what was our duty." ' [4] There is certainly no hint of works of supererogation here, but quite the reverse.

The apostle Paul can speak of himself, after years of unflagging devotion to Christ, as the chief of sinners.[5] The apostle John stands alongside those to whom he writes as he asserts, 'If we say we have no sin, we deceive ourselves and the truth is not in us.' [6] But if sin is thus always a fact, then our good works are themselves tainted by this continuing sinfulness, and thus

[4] Lk. 17:9f.   [5] 1Tim. 1:15.   [6] 1 Jn. 1:8.

become acceptable to God only because they are offered through Christ our Saviour. Note how Paul assesses the situation. Writing to the Corinthians he considers his own present position and attainments, which were indeed notable. Yet he goes on to confess, 'But by the grace of God I am what I am, and his grace toward me was not in vain. On the contrary, I worked harder than any of them, though it was not I, but the grace of God which is with me.' [7]

In any event none of us can act for his brother. There is no transference of merit from one believer to another in the pages of the New Testament. In the imagery of the parable of the Ten Virgins [8] the five wise virgins are unable to share the oil which they have provided for their lamps with the foolish who are unready, and whose lamps have gone out. In the more explicit statement of the apostle Paul, 'So each of us shall give account of himself to God.' [9]

An appeal is made to the Lord's promise to His disciples 'Whatever you bind on earth shall be bound in heaven: and whatever you loose on earth shall be loosed in heaven.' [1] Here, it is claimed, is divine sanction for the authority of the Church to bind in terms of discipline and to loose in terms of indulgence. Such binding and loosing is done on earth, but it is ratified by God in heaven.

But even a cursory glance at the context will show how baseless is the appeal to this verse to support the elaborate doctrine of indulgences. The Lord is dealing with the practical problem of human relationships within the Church. Here is a Christian who has been injured in some way by a fellow member of the Church. What is he to do in such a situation? The Lord gives precise instructions. He is first of all to deal privately with the offender. If the latter persists in his attitude, the injured one must take one or two other Christians so that they may be witnesses of the issue involved. If however this proves fruitless, appeal must be made to the Church. If in face of this final appeal the offender remains obstinate, and refuses to make

[7] 1 Cor. 15:10.   [8] Mt. 25:1–13.   [9] Rom. 14:12.
[1] Mt. 18:18.

149

amends, then discipline is to be applied. He is to be treated as a heathen and a publican, that is to say, he is to be excluded from communion. Such an act of discipline by the Church will however be ratified by God, who has given powers of discipline to His Church. So too, He will also ratify their suspension of the sentence when the man shows signs of penitence.

But surely all this is just the position we have already seen in Corinth. The persistent offender who refuses to acknowledge his sin is to be excommunicated; but if he turns in penitence he is to be restored. But this simply means that the Church has the right to impose a penalty by way of discipline, in order to bring a man to repentance, and in order to maintain the purity of the Church. It is therefore a Church penalty which is imposed, and so the indulgence is likewise the remission of that same Church penalty.

This does not mean that the penalty of excommunication is to be treated lightly. Indeed it is one of the solemn consequences of sin in that the offender is shut off from the privileges of fellowship with God's people, and shut out from meeting with them at the Lord's Table. His exclusion by the Church is all the more serious in that it reflects the discipline of God. So too, restoration by the Church to communion is to be valued as it leads to the blessings of fellowship with the people of God and also echoes God's own word of restoration and favour.

But this kind of indulgence has nothing to do with the Roman Catholic practice. After all the one to whom an indulgence is offered by Rome cannot be one who is excommunicated. In order to benefit from an indulgence he would need to be in a state of grace, which could not be so if he were under the ban of the Church. To return to the position where he would be ready to receive such an indulgence, he would need the ban lifted, so that he might go to the priest for absolution. In short, the indulgence of New Testament discipline applies to the excommunicated one, while the Roman Catholic indulgence must, in the nature of the case, be applied only to one who is in communion. For Rome the one kind of indulgence would have to precede the other. But clearly they are of a different kind altogether and the appeal to Matthew 18 falls to the ground.

The New Testament knows only one treasury of merit, and that is the righteousness of Christ. To set anything of human merit alongside His perfect righteousness is nothing less than an affront to the Son of God. But this righteousness is not a treasury which is under the control of man. To Christ every believer has access. His constant invitation is 'Come to me, all who labour and are heavy laden'; [2] and, as He points us to the Father, He says 'I am the way'.[3] The sinner's first approach to the Father is through Christ upon whose righteousness alone he relics. But every subsequent approach is on the same terms. It is the merits of Christ, the righteousness of his Saviour, that he pleads. Confident that this righteousness is accepted he has no need to have recourse to the supposed merits of any other. He rejects emphatically the alleged benefits of an indulgence whose very basis he sees to be a reflection on the perfection of his Saviour's work, and on the completeness of the Father's pardon.

[2] Mt. 11:28.   [3] Jn. 14:6.

15

Death and the hereafter

Death is an inescapable fact of which all must take account. We may try to forget it or to dismiss it with a joke; but inevitably there come times when it forces its way into the forefront of our thinking. It may be through the sobering realization that we too must die, or it may be through the crushing sorrow of bereavement. At such times questions crowd in with an agonizing insistence. Faced with the uncertainties of the future, men want desperately to know what lies beyond the grave.

It is here that the Christian message rings with such an assured note of hope. The gospel of Christ is not one that is concerned only with this life. Indeed, said Paul, 'If for this life only we have hoped in Christ, we are of all men most to be pitied.'[1] But our hope reaches beyond the grave, for Christ has taken the sting from death by His resurrection from the dead. It is this which sweeps the apostle to such a high point of triumphant exultation as he cries, 'O death, where is thy victory? O death, where is thy sting? . . . Thanks be to God, who gives us the victory through our Lord Jesus Christ.'[2]

Now no-one would accuse the Church of Rome of ignoring death, for in her teaching she treats it as a matter of great importance. This is reflected, on the one hand, in the deep concern that a priest should be summoned in times of serious illness and, on the other, in the prominence given to the practice of offering requiem masses for the repose of the souls of the departed. The presence of the priest when a person is dangerously ill is, of course, in order that he might administer

[1] 1 Cor. 15–19.   [2] 1 Cor 15:55, 57.

152

extreme unction; while the justification of the requiem mass is the doctrine of purgatory. We must therefore examine these two aspects of Roman Catholic dogma, which are closely related in that they are dealing with the problems which are encountered in face of death.

It is claimed that extreme unction is a true and proper sacrament instituted by Christ and, indeed, the Council of Trent anathematized those who would deny this – 'This sacred anointing of the sick was instituted by Christ our Lord as truly and properly a sacrament of the New Law.' [3] As far as the sacramental character of the ordinance is concerned, it is maintained that oil constitutes the 'matter' while the prayer of the priest is the 'form'. The aim in view in the administration is the preparation for death. Thus Rome teaches, not only that the anointing gives grace to help the dying man in his last struggle, but that it also effects remission of mortal and of venial sins, and in addition removes the temporal consequences of sins – 'For the thing signified is the grace of the Holy Spirit whose anointing takes away the sins if there be any still to be expiated, and also the remains of sin.' [4]

There are of course qualifications. Normally a person must be in a state of grace, that is to say, he must not be in a condition of impenitence. If, however, he is not in a fit state to exercise either contrition, or even attrition with its accompanying confession, then, if his normal attitude was one of attrition rather than deliberate sinfulness, this is acceptable. As far as the removal of the consequences of sin is concerned, this is not absolute but corresponds 'to the intensity of charity and penance in the recipient'.[5]

But all this elaboration founders on some very obvious facts. In the first place there is not the slightest hint in the New Testament that Christ instituted such an ordinance. Trent finds it prefigured in the Gospels where the disciples 'anointed with oil many that were sick'.[6] But we need only to complete the verse to see that the object of the anointing was not preparation

[3] Council of Trent, Fourteenth Session, ch. I.   [4] *Ibid.*, ch II.
[5] Ludwig Ott, *op. cit.*, p. 448.   [6] Mk. 6:13.

for death but quite the reverse, for Mark adds that they 'healed them'.

The main verse upon which reliance is placed is James's word to those who are sick.[7] But again the text cited simply will not bear the weight that is placed upon it. As in Mark, it is not death which is in view here at all, but restoration. It is the man himself who summons the presbyters who come and anoint him. Nor, indeed, is it the oil to which efficacy is accorded, but prayer. It is the 'prayer of faith' which saves the sick, and as a result he is raised up. But it would be a very fanciful piece of interpretation to suggest that this means he is raised up to heaven! It quite obviously speaks of healing and restoration to health. Coupled with this gift of healing is the forgiveness of sins, which of course accords with the situation in which the man has sought the blessing of God. In the apostolic practice a Christian who is sick seeks healing and, as always, forgiveness from the Lord. But the Roman Catholic unction is something completely different, for it is administered only when the likelihood is that the person will die. It has death in view, not life.

In spite of such preparation for death, however, there still remains the grim fact of purgatory. A man after all may die without having the opportunity of calling the priest, so that, while he may still die in a state of grace, his venial sins and the temporal consequences of mortal sin remain to be expiated. Indeed, as we have seen, in extreme unction the temporal consequences are removed only in accordance with the degree of 'charity and penance' exercised by him. Hence, even with unction, he may still have to face some of these consequences beyond the grave, and thus for him, too, there lie ahead the purifying fires of purgatory.

In view of misunderstanding in many minds, it should be stressed that Rome does not declare purgatory to be the goal of all who die. For any who die in mortal sin, and in a state of impenitence, death marks the end of their time of probation and hell is their portion. For those who die in a state of perfect holiness there is the immediate entry into heaven. To the latter

[7] Jas. 5:14.

class would belong the martyrs whose blood would be considered as their final purification. But in practice those who enter heaven immediately are a tiny minority, whereas the great majority who die in a state of grace must endure the pains of purgatory.

The Council of Florence clearly enunciated the doctrine. 'If any have departed this life in penitence and love of God, before they have made satisfaction for their sins of omission and commission by fruits worthy of repentance their souls are purified after death by purgatorial punishments.' This was confirmed by the Council of Trent which, while admitting that there were abuses in the presentation of the dogma, still maintained that 'there is a Purgatory and that the souls detained in it are benefited by the prayers of the faithful and especially by the sacrifice of the altar'.[8] Vatican II's Decree on the Church refers to those who, 'their life now over, are undergoing purification'.[9] While the councils do not endorse the view of many Roman Catholic theologians that purgatory implies fire, they do speak of 'purifying punishments'. Thus the process involves suffering, and indeed the suffering has been compared to the suffering of hell itself.

Now in a sense we have already replied to this earlier, in our stress on the perfection of Christ's sacrifice and on the completeness of God's forgiveness. Christ's death met to the full the demands of God's justice, and because of this God freely and fully forgives those who trust in Christ. To demand a further satisfaction in purgatory is to say, either that the satisfaction offered by Christ was insufficient, or that the Father is exacting further punishment although the penalty has already been borne. Purgatory, in other words, denies either the perfection of Christ's atonement, or the justice of God. 'The blood of Jesus Christ his Son cleanseth us from all sin',[1] and it is nothing less than an affront to the Son of God to suggest that further purging is needed. 'God put forward (Christ) as an expiation by his blood, to be received by faith.'[2] Are we then to say that the

8 Twenty-fifth Session, Decree on Purgatory.
9 VII:49.   1 1 Jn. 1:7.   2 Rom. 3:25.

propitiation has been rejected or, even worse, that it has been accepted and yet God still requires more? For it is important to note that it is not just the purifying of the sinner which is involved, but the satisfaction which must be offered to God Himself.

Rome attempts to justify her teaching by appeal to the apocryphal book of 2 Maccabees. The occasion was the discovery of symbols of idolatrous worship under the clothes of some Jewish soldiers who had died in battle. Judas sent money to Jerusalem for sacrifice to be offered for the sins of the dead and the comment is added 'It is therefore a holy and wholesome thought to pray for the dead, that they may be loosed from sins.' [3] But apart from the whole question of the value of the appeal to an apocryphal book, this passage proves too much! These men having died in idolatry were guilty, by Roman Catholic standards, of a mortal sin, and as such faced the penalty of hell, for purgatory is only for those who die in penitence and the love of God. If Rome must appeal to the apocrypha then she would find a less contradictory position in Wisdom, 'But the souls of the righteous are in the hand of God: and no torment will ever touch them . . . but they are at peace.' [4]

Returning, however, to the sure ground of the New Testament Scriptures, Rome quotes Paul's words concerning the testing which Christian teachers will face in the last day: 'And the fire will test what sort of work each one has done.' [5] But an examination of the context will show that this has nothing at all to do with purgatory. Paul is speaking about the work of God's ministers, as is acknowledged by the introductory word placed, in the Douay Version, at the beginning of the chapter. The question at issue is the quality of the work which they do, and the permanence of its fruits. The day which shall bring to light the character of this work is not the day of their death, but 'the day of the Lord', which in the New Testament, of course, means the day of judgment. The burning itself is a destructive

[3] 2 Macc. 12:46 (Vulgate).
[4] Wisdom 3:1–3.   [5] 1 Cor. 3:13.

156

one, but it is noteworthy that it is the work of the minister that is the object. Here, in short, is a warning to the man called to the task of the Christian ministry. His work that he does in Christ's name will one day be tested. If it is inferior in quality it will be rejected. Only if it is of enduring value will it be accepted. To have one's life work rejected is indeed to 'suffer loss', even though one has the comfort that the fiery judgment of the last day may destroy the work while the worker himself, saved by the blood of Christ, is spared.

Appeal is made to Peter's words concerning 'the spirits in prison' [6] to whom Christ preached. But again the context is the decisive voice. Peter specifically mentions the class of people to whom he refers. They were those who were disobedient in the days of Noah. We might wonder why Peter should select this small group until we recall his analogy, culled doubtless from the Lord's words,[7] between the days of Noah and the day of final judgment.[8] The parallel is as follows. Noah preached; men disobeyed; they were judged: so Christ preaches; men reject; and are condemned. Hence the preaching to the spirits in prison is that which Christ did through the agency of Noah, and in confirmation of this is the fact that Christ did this 'in the spirit'. We freely admit that this is a most difficult passage, but we would suggest that only someone wanting to establish a theory could argue from the preaching to the restricted group of spirits in prison, to the necessity of purification after death for the great majority of the people of God.

Another scripture used is the word of the Lord. 'Make friends quickly with your accuser, while you are going with him to court, lest your accuser hand you over to the judge, and the judge to the guard, and you be put in prison; truly I say to you, you will never get out till you have paid the last penny.' [9] Now clearly this is another difficult passage, and indeed, if the Roman Catholic rule were true that the unanimous consent of the Fathers is necessary for a true interpretation, then we would have to pass it by! But in any case it says nothing about purgatory. On the contrary the judgment to which Christ referred

[6] 1 Pet. 3:19.   [7] Mt. 24:37.   [8] 2 Pet. 2:4f.
[9] Mt. 5:25f.

in verse 22 is not the fire of purgatory but 'hell fire'. Hence if we take the 'judge' here to be God, then surely the judgment to be dreaded in this context is hell. But in that case the word about paying the last penny is simply a vivid way of declaring the hopelessness of the position, for from hell there is no deliverance.

Another very doubtful basis for the dogma is found in Christ's warning on the peril of sinning against the Holy Spirit. Such a sin, He said, shall not be forgiven 'either in this age or in the age to come'.[1] Here, Dr Ott claims, the Lord 'leaves open the possibility that sins are forgiven not only in this world but in the world to come'.[2] But that this is a very dubious inference can be seen by looking at the account given by Mark and Luke of this saying.[3] They do not mention 'the age to come' but simply stress the unpardonable character of the sin. Hence in Matthew's account we must surely see only the Lord's very emphatic stress on this solemn fact, without trying to read into it something else which simply is not there. It is always a risky procedure to argue from a man's vigorous refusal at some point that he may have other concessions in mind.

It is no wonder that Dr Ott has to admit that 'the main proof for the existence of the cleansing fire lies in the testimony of the Fathers'[4] for the scriptural justification presented is very tenuous indeed. But, on the other hand, the Scriptures which reject the dogma do not need any manipulation or special pleading, for they bear clearly and openly their testimony to a very different prospect for the believer after death.

The Lord speaks such a word of assurance, 'Truly, truly, I say to you, he who hears my word and believes him who sent me, has eternal life; he does not come into judgment, but has passed from death to life.'[5] Of Lazarus He declares that his condition after death is one of comfort, as he is carried by the angels, not to the terrors of purgatory, but to Abraham's bosom.[6] To the dying thief He gives a clear promise of an

[1] Mt. 12:32.
[2] *Op. cit.*, p. 483.
[3] Mk. 3:28–30; Lk. 12:10.
[4] *Op. cit.*, p. 484.
[5] Jn. 5:24.
[6] Lk. 16:19–31.

immediate entry into bliss: 'Truly, I say to you today you will be with me in Paradise.' [7] And lest any one should try to insert purgatory into paradise, it is important to notice the vital phrase in the promise – the thief is that day to be 'with Christ' and quite obviously Christ was not going to endure some purifying fire.

The apostles simply echo the words of Christ. For Paul, 'to live is Christ; and to die is gain'.[8] He has a 'desire to depart and be with Christ, for that is far better'.[9] He is confident that to be 'away from the body' is 'to be at home with the Lord'.[1] Nor is this confidence confined to his own destiny. For every Christian, death has lost its sting.[2] John on Patmos hears a divine confirmation of these confidently expressed hopes: 'I heard a voice from heaven, saying, "Write this: Blessed are the dead who die in the Lord henceforth." "Blessed indeed," says the Spirit, "that they may rest from their labours, for their deeds follow them!"' [3]

The history of the dogma has been one of sorry corruption in the Church. The gross commercialization of the sixteenth-century hawker of indulgences may be, in this country at least, a thing of the past. Yet it is a fact that the financial element still enters, either in terms of a legacy left for the purpose of having requiem masses said for the deliverance of the soul from purgatory, or of an offering made by the bereaved relatives for the same purpose. But surely, if Pope or priest have the power of easing such suffering, they should not require a payment. Rome may reply that this is a parody of their position, for the payment is rather in terms of an offering by the faithful. But we must then ask a further question. Does the Church know infallibly how long the sufferer will be in purgatory? The answer to this of course is in the negative. But in that case the money received – call it payment, or offering, or what you will – is given for a requiem for a soul who even in Rome's teaching may already be free.

Purgatory is one dogma of Rome about which it is hard not

[7] Lk. 23:43. [8] Phil. 1:21. [9] Phil. 1–23.
[1] 2 Cor. 5:8. [2] 1 Cor. 15:55. [3] Rev. 14:13.

159

to feel indignant. Here is a figment of the ecclesiastical imagination which has not a shred of solid scriptural evidence to support it, and which yet does so much to rob Christians of the hope that should be theirs. The Lord says to His disciples, 'Let not your hearts be troubled'.[4] But how can a Christian avoid being troubled if death means an entry, not into the Saviour's presence, but into an agony as bad as hell even if not as enduring? Paul urges the Thessalonians not to sorrow for their dead like the pagans who have no hope.[5] But how can one fail to mourn at the prospect of appalling suffering for a loved one? Purgatory brings a shadow to the death bed, and casts that shadow still over the lives of those left behind. What a contrast to the biblical pattern where the believer faces the end with the calm assurance of an immediate entry into paradise, and where those who mourn are enabled to dry their tears, as they rejoice in the bliss which their loved one already enjoys in the presence of Christ.

[4] Jn. 14:1.   [5] 1 Thes. 4:12ff.

16

Can we be sure?

In the Epistle to the Romans the apostle Paul faces what may be called the most fundamental issue of all: how may a man be justified? Given God in all His holiness, and man in his sin, how can such a sinner stand before such a holy God and be accepted? It was no mere academic issue for Paul, for he had tried hard to solve the problem in his days of earnest legalism, and he had found the solution only when he had met with Christ. The answer to the question is clearly of supreme importance, and it is at precisely this point that the divergence of Rome and the Reformed Churches is seen in its most acute form. Yet it is at this point above all that the man who is in earnest about his standing before God desires a clear reply.

When we turn to the Bible we are confronted at the outset with a constant emphasis on the grace of God. The Bible is essentially God-centred. When it speaks of creation it is in relation to the power and majesty of the Creator. When it deals with history the stress is on the sovereign control of God Almighty. When it speaks of human life it is the providence of God which is set forth. And when it deals with the work of redemption the same stress is present. The purpose to redeem had its origin in the will of God.[1] The love which sent the Saviour was His.[2] The power which raises the sinner to new life is His.[3] The ultimate aim in the work of salvation is the glory of God. We can recall the refrain in Paul's Epistle to the Ephesians where he sees God's purpose that we might be 'to the praise of his glory'.[4]

[1] Rom. 8:28–30; Eph. 1:4–11.   [2] Jn. 3:16; Rom. 5:8f.
[3] Eph. 2:4–7.   [4] Eph. 1:6, 12, 14.

But if God is to receive all the glory, then clearly there is no room for human pride or boasting. Indeed the apostle Paul would say that the whole plan of salvation is designed by God to silence all such human claims. 'Then what becomes of our boasting?' he asks; and he replies, 'It is excluded. On what principle? On the principle of works? No, but on the principle of faith.'[5] In similar vein he writes to the Ephesians, 'For by grace you have been saved through faith; and this is not your own doing, it is the gift of God – not because of works, lest any man should boast.'[6] His own testimony echoes this. 'But, by the grace of God, I am what I am.'[7] 'Far be it from me to glory except in the cross of our Lord Jesus Christ.'[8]

Thus, not only the forgiveness of sins but even man's response in repentance and faith is declared to be due to the grace of God. The Lord Himself emphasized man's inability to turn himself. 'No one can come to me except the Father who sent me draws him.'[9] The apostle Peter maintains that the divine purpose for the risen Christ is that He should 'give repentance to Israel and forgiveness of sins';[1] and the disciples later rejoice in this gift of 'repentance unto life'.[2] The apostle Paul speaks of faith likewise as 'the gift of God',[3] an echo of his report of his missionary work on another occasion that God 'had opened a door of faith to the Gentiles'.[4]

Now linked to this stress on the grace of God there is a corresponding stress on faith. If it is 'by grace' that we are saved, in that we are utterly dependent on the grace of God, then it is also true that it is 'through faith'. The sinner comes with empty hands to receive the blessings which God gives. He may ask, like the Philippian gaoler, 'What must I do to be saved?' But the reply will simply be 'Believe in the Lord Jesus, and you will be saved.'[5] It is by faith alone that we are justified.[6]

But what does it mean to be justified? The answer to this

[5] Rom. 3:27. [6] Eph. 2:8f. [7] 1 Cor. 15:10.
[8] Gal. 6:14. [9] Jn. 6:44. [1] Acts 5:31.
[2] Acts 11:18. [3] Eph. 2:8. [4] Acts 14:27.
[5] Acts 16:30f. [6] Rom. 5:1.

162

question is the theme of Paul's letter to the Romans. In the opening chapters he shows man as he is before God, and the climax is reached in his sweeping indictment that the whole world is held accountable before God.[7] But God has an answer to man's desperate plight, and it is in the gospel. Christ is set forth as the only righteous One. His righteousness may be viewed from two aspects. Positively He kept the law, in that He offered a perfect and unsullied obedience to His Father. Negatively He bore the penalty that was due to those who had broken God's law. Thus He is the 'propitiation', the sacrifice provided by God Himself. In all this He was acting as the representative of His people. 'But he was wounded for our transgressions, he was bruised for our iniquities; upon him was the chastisement that made us whole, and with his stripes we are healed.'[8] He 'himself, bore our sins in his body on the tree'.[9] 'For our sakes he (i.e. God) made him to be sin who knew no sin.'[1]

Thus in the cross God's justice is vindicated, for the full penalty of death falls upon sin when the blow falls upon the lamb of God 'who takes away the sin of the world'.[2] Hence when, for Christ's sake, God receives the ungodly, pardoning his sins, and accounting him righteous, it is 'to prove at the present time that he himself is righteous and that he justifies him who has faith in Jesus'.[3] The rebel who was under the judgment of God is freely received, because that judgment which was his due has fallen upon another. 'Christ redeemed us from the curse of the law, having become a curse for us.'[4]

Now it is precisely at this vital point in the Christian message that Roman dogma seriously obscures the position. By denying the Reformers' emphasis on 'faith alone' the Council of Trent inevitably qualifies its own stress on the grace of God. Of course we freely admit that Rome acknowledges the supreme importance of the grace of God. A Church which honours the name of the great Augustine could hardly fail to emphasize the grace

[7] Rom. 3:19.   [8] Is. 53:5.   [9] 1 Pet. 2:24.
[1] 2 Cor. 5:21.   [2] Jn. 1:29.   [3] Rom. 3:26.
[4] Gal. 3:13.

of God in salvation. Yet at the same time, by introducing the idea of human effort and thus denying the principle of 'faith alone', Rome reduces the role of the grace of God. Once we view man as working along with God we have denied the basic biblical contention that it is by grace that we are justified. A junior partner in a firm may be dependent on the capital of his senior, but he has his own vital contribution to make which, though small, is one for which he can take credit. The man, then, who sees himself as a partner in the work of salvation is opening the sluice-gates to the pride which since Eden has proved our undoing.

Behind Rome's readiness to accept man's freedom and ability to perform good works is her failure to receive the biblical declaration concerning man in sin. Original righteousness, which Adam had before the fall, consisted according to Rome in a supernatural gift. The fall meant a loss of this sanctifying grace. Man therefore, although he is a sinner and in need of grace, is yet free to turn to God and to prepare himself for justification. 'The sinner can and must prepare himself by the help of actual grace for the reception of the grace by which he is justified.' [5] Hence Rome rejects the position that man's nature was completely corrupted by Adam's sin. The canons of the Council of Trent are quite emphatic on this score: 'If anyone shall say that the sinner is justified by faith alone, meaning that nothing else is required to co-operate in order to obtain the grace of justification, and that it is not in any way necessary that he be prepared and disposed by the action of his own will – let him be accursed.' [6]

But what then are we to make of the biblical verdict on man? He is declared to be spiritually blind. 'The god of this world hath blinded the minds of unbelievers, to keep them from seeing the light of the gospel of the glory of Christ, who is the likeness of God.' [7] So too, man is ignorant and, indeed, is incapable in his natural state of receiving spiritual truth. In face of the Roman Catholic position that 'even in the fallen

[5] Ludwig Ott, *Fundamentals of Catholic Dogma*, p. 252.
[6] *Canons Concerning Justification*, no. 9.   [7] 2 Cor. 4:4.

state, man can, by his natural intellectual power, know religious and moral truths',[8] the apostle Paul replies with vigour: 'The unspiritual man does not receive the gifts of the Spirit of God, for they are folly to him, and he is not able to understand them because they are spiritually discerned.'[9] Man in his blindness and ignorance is also in bondage. He is a slave who needs to be set free. 'You who were once slaves of sin . . . having been set free from sin, have become slaves of righteousness.'[1] Paul indeed goes even further and declares man in his fallen state to be spiritually dead.[2] It is no wonder then that the Scripture maintains that 'they who are in the flesh cannot please God'.[3] The prophetic word is constantly reinforced. 'We have all become like one who is unclean, and all our righteous deeds are like a polluted garment. We all fade like a leaf, and our iniquities like the wind take us away.'[4]

To the objection that this makes man incapable of hearing and responding to the gospel, we reply with the biblical testimony that both hearing and responding are due to the grace of God alone. Paul, having pronounced man to be dead in sins, speaks also of the miracle of renewal. It was when you were dead, he says, that God gave you life.[5] Just as the life-giving word of Christ called Lazarus from the tomb, so the gospel, applied powerfully by the Spirit of God, calls the sinner from the death of sin to the life of righteousness. Hence his very willingness to turn and believe is ascribed by Paul to God's work in him.[6]

But Rome continues further to confuse the mind of the seeker. Having opened the door for human effort, and so derogated from the grace of God, she adds to the difficulty with her view of justification. Rejecting the Reformers' contention that justification is essentially a declaration by the Judge, by which He pronounces the sinner righteous, she contends for the position that to justify means rather to make righteous. Refusing the position that the perfect righteousness of Christ is imputed

[8] Ludwig Ott, *op. cit.*, p. 233.   [9] 1 Cor. 2:14.
[1] Rom. 6:17f.   [2] Eph. 2:1.   [3] Rom. 8:8.
[4] Is. 64:6.   [5] Eph. 2:5.   [6] Phil. 2:13.

to the sinner, she maintains, rather, that righteousness is infused into, or imparted to, the sinner by God. This takes place in baptism which is 'the instrumental cause' of justification, 'without which no man was ever justified'.[7] But this means that, while it is in a sense God's righteousness, it is in a sense also man's. Hence the ground of man's justification is the righteousness which he himself has, instead of the perfect righteousness of Christ. Instead of the gloriously objective declaration of the finished work of Christ, and the spotless righteousness of Christ, he is left with his own subjective condition as the grounds of his acceptance.

It is no wonder, therefore, that he is left without assurance that he is truly in a state of grace. How can he be sure that this righteousness which he possesses is a sufficient ground, especially when he is only too aware of his own unrighteousness and sin? Rome would reply that he cannot be sure, and indeed that he should not expect to be sure, for such a claim to assurance is nothing less than presumption. He may hope that he is accepted, but he cannot go further than that. 'If one considers his own weakness and his defective disposition, he may well be fearful and anxious as to his state of grace, as nobody knows with the certainty of faith, which permits of no error, that he has achieved the grace of God.'[8]

But what then are we to say to Paul's confidence, 'For I know whom I have believed and I am sure that he is able to guard until that Day what has been entrusted to me.'[9] Was Paul encouraging presumption when he wrote to the Philippians, 'And I am sure that he who began a good work in you will bring it to completion at the day of Jesus Christ.'[1] Was John similarly guilty when he declared that his purpose in writing his Epistle was that 'you who believe in the name of the Son of God may know that you have eternal life'?[2]

The verdict of Scripture is plain, and it is confirmed in experience. Once let man claim any part in his salvation, and he

[7] Council of Trent Sixth Session, Ch. VII.
[8] Ludwig Ott, *op. cit.*, p. 262.
[9] 2 Tim. 1:12.   [1] Phil. 1:6.   [2] 1 Jn. 5:13.

ends in a morass of self-effort and doubt. Accept the biblical emphasis that the grace of God is the sole and undisputed source of our salvation, and not only is human pride excluded, but humble confidence is begotten. Yield to the Roman Catholic position that grace in this context is not so much the goodwill of God, who for Christ's sake freely forgives the sinner, but is rather 'a divine quality inhering in the soul'[3] – yield here and in Luther's words, one is on the shifting sands of one's own righteousness. But once let a sinner pin all his hopes on the righteousness of Christ, let him, as Augustine did long ago, listen to the call of the apostle to 'put on the Lord Jesus Christ',[4] let him be thus clothed with the righteousness of Christ, and he will stand secure, not only now, but in the day of judgment.

Rome will object that all this makes faith a mere empty reaction, and makes justification a purely external act of God which bears no relation to the character of the sinner. But surely the faith of which the Scriptures speak is no mere nod of assent to certain propositions. It is rather personal trust in the Son of God. Such faith, while it is 'faith alone', does not, as Calvin pointed out, remain alone. True faith will show itself in good works. But it is one thing to say that good works are the outcome of faith; it is quite another to make faith itself a good work. The fruit of the tree must not be made into the root! So too the justification of the sinner, while it is the declaration of the Judge, leads inevitably to the life of holiness. When a man who has rebelled against his country receives an amnesty, he will then begin to live as a good citizen. But his pardon must be clear and decisive or he can have no confidence in his return to his old home. So too the sinner is called to a life of holiness. But it is only when his justification is a clear verdict of the Judge that he can apply himself by the grace of God to those good works which God had in mind when He pardoned him.[5]

It is surely significant, and indeed a striking comment on Paul's stress on 'faith alone', that he faced a similar objection. There were those, apparently, who were objecting to his gospel

---

[3] Ludwig Ott, *op. cit.*, p. 255.
[4] Rom. 13:14. [5] Eph. 2:9f.

and asking 'Are we to continue in sin, that grace may abound?' [6] Surely, some would maintain, Paul's denial of human merit, and his emphasis on faith alone, will lead to carelessness. If an act of faith is sufficient, what is to hinder a man from performing this requirement, and then living as he pleases? Paul wholeheartedly repudiates such an idea; but in doing so he does not retract one whit his insistence on faith alone. He would reply that the faith of a man who can reason thus is no faith at all. True saving faith is essentially fruitful. To be united to Christ is to be impelled to live a life of holiness. To believe in Christ, in other words, is not simply to make an outward profession. It is to believe with the heart in the Saviour.

To recall Martin Luther will possibly, in the context of this book, conjure up the picture of his great protest against indulgences as he nailed his theses to the door of the castle Church at Wittenberg, or as he stood at the Diet of Worms with his stirring confession 'Here I stand; I can do no other'. But it might be better to go back to an earlier point, and see Luther in his cell in the monastery at Erfurt, for it is there that we can see the controversy, not simply as an academic discussion, but as a spiritual struggle in the heart of an earnest seeker after God.

Luther's agonizing question was the one which Augustine had faced, and which Paul had faced. How may a man be righteous before God? It was in order to try and achieve this righteousness that he had abandoned his legal career to become a monk. It was this same quest which drove him to the austerities with which he nearly wrecked himself physically. It was his desperate longing for pardon which drove him so frequently to the confessional that he even wearied his confessor. But all this, and much more, left him, as it had left the apostle Paul, still in the darkness. The other monks might look on him as the young saint of Erfurt; but he knew himself to be only a sinner, guilty, lost and helpless. But peace came to his troubled soul. The word of the gospel stood out in letters of light, 'The righteous shall live by faith.' Luther turned from his own efforts

[6] Rom. 6:1.

and rested only on the righteousness of Christ. For Christ's sake he knew himself to be forgiven. Being justified by faith he had peace with God. It is in that experience that we see mirrored not only the basic controversy between Rome and the Reformed Churches; we see also the issue of life and death, of heaven and hell, which confronts each one of us.

Bibliography

(Roman Catholic works are marked *)

Traditional Catholicism

G. C. Berkouwer, *The Conflict with Rome* (Presbyterian & Reformed Publishing Co., 1958).
W. S. Kerr, *A Handbook on the Papacy* (Marshall, Morgan & Scott, 1962).
G. Miegge, *The Virgin Mary* (Lutterworth, 1961).
* L. Ott, *Fundamentals of Catholic Dogma* (Mercier Press, 1962).
* K. Rahner (Ed.), *The Teaching of the Catholic Church* (Mercier Press, 1966).
* J. Neuner and J. Dupuis (Eds), *The Christian Faith* (Mercier Press, 1973).
G. Salmon, *The Infallibility of the Church* (John Murray, 1914; Abridged edition, 1953).
V. Subilia, *The Problem of Catholicism* (SCM, 1964).

The New Catholicism

G. C. Berkouwer, *The Second Vatican Council and the New Catholicism* (Eerdmans, 1965).
* A. M. J. Kloosterman, *Contemporary Catholicism* (Collins, 1972).
* H. Küng, *The Church* (Burns & Oates, 1967); *Structures* (Burns & Oates, 1965); *Justification* (Burns & Oates, 1964); *Infallible?* (Collins, 1971); *Why Priests?* (Collins, 1972).
D. F. Wells, *Revolution in Rome* (Tyndale Press, 1973).

Catholic Pentecostalism

* K. and D. Ranaghan, *Catholic Pentecostals* (Paulist Press, 1969).
* S. Tugwell, *Did You Receive the Spirit?* (Darton, Longman & Todd, 1972).
* T. Flynn, *The Charismatic Renewal and the Irish Experience* (Hodder & Stoughton, 1974).

Vatican I

* C. Butler, *The First Vatican Council* (Collins, 1962).

Vatican II

* W. M. Abbott and J. Gallagher (Eds), *The Documents of Vatican II* (Geoffrey Chapman, 1966).
* Y. Congar, O.P.; H. Küng and D. O'Hanlon, S.J. (Eds), *Council Speeches of Vatican II* (Sheed & Ward, 1964).
* K. McNamara (Ed.), *Vatican II: The Constitution on the Church* (Geoffrey Chapman, 1968).

Short Glossary of Roman Catholic Terms

Adjutrix — a female assistant.

Auxiliatrix — a female helper. Both these terms are titles given to the Virgin Mary.

Bull — from the Latin *bulla* the seal which is attached to the document – a solemn papal mandate.

Encyclical — a letter from the Pope to all the bishops in communion with him.

Hierarchy — from the Greek word *hiereus* meaning priest – the term means rule by priests and is applied to the graded structure of the priestly organization of the Roman Catholic Church.

Magisterium — from the Latin *magister*, a teacher, it is the title given to the teaching authority of the Church.

Mediatrix — female mediator – a title given to the Virgin Mary.

Motu Proprio — from the Latin, meaning 'by his own motion'. It refers to a letter sent out in the Pope's own name without reference to any other official, and indicating some rule to be observed.

Pontiff — from the Latin *Pontifex Maximus*, 'the Chief Priest' – the old title used in pagan Roman religion.

Venial — pardonable – referring to sins which are not considered to be mortal (*i.e.* 'killing') sins which deprive a person of sanctifying grace.

Revolution in Rome

DAVID F. WELLS

An examination of the trends of progressive and conservative Roman Catholic theology in the light of Vatican II.

128 pp.

Inter-Varsity Press

The clockwork image

DONALD M. MacKAY

Does science rule out the possibility of God's existence?
Are we, after all, nothing but machines?

112 pp.

Inter-Varsity Press